LIFE IN CHRIST
Daily Devotional Journal

CJ COUSINS

WESTBOW
PRESS®
A DIVISION OF THOMAS NELSON
& ZONDERVAN

Copyright © 2021 CJ Cousins.

All rights reserved. No part of this book may be used or reproduced by any means, graphic, electronic, or mechanical, including photocopying, recording, taping or by any information storage retrieval system without the written permission of the author except in the case of brief quotations embodied in critical articles and reviews.

WestBow Press books may be ordered through booksellers or by contacting:

WestBow Press
A Division of Thomas Nelson & Zondervan
1663 Liberty Drive
Bloomington, IN 47403
www.westbowpress.com
844-714-3454

Because of the dynamic nature of the Internet, any web addresses or links contained in this book may have changed since publication and may no longer be valid. The views expressed in this work are solely those of the author and do not necessarily reflect the views of the publisher, and the publisher hereby disclaims any responsibility for them.

Any people depicted in stock imagery provided by Getty Images are models, and such images are being used for illustrative purposes only. Certain stock imagery © Getty Images.

Scripture taken from the New King James Version® Copyright © 1982 by Thomas Nelson. Used by permission. All rights reserved.

ISBN: 978-1-6642-0812-4 (sc)
ISBN: 978-1-6642-0813-1 (e)

Library of Congress Control Number: 2020919513

Print information available on the last page.

WestBow Press rev. date: 03/18/2021

CONTENTS

Introduction ix

Chapter 1 Jesus Is Our Model 1
Chapter 2 See the Story with a Gospel Lens.............. 7
Chapter 3 How to Use This Journal 13

Conclusion 29

This book is dedicated to my grandmother Hazel Barns, who was affectionately known as "Mamita". Her life of loving devotion to Christ that I witnessed, until she went to sleep in Him at age 101, has inspired this work.

This book is also dedicated to Ada Mendez, whom I worked with at the Dean's Office of the seminary at Andrews University. Our conversations at the office about your experience with Jesus when using the early developing stages of this daily devotional journal, the tears of joy in Him you shed and the presence of the Holy Spirit as we shared our insights from the journal entries have never left my mind.

I also dedicate this work to my mother, Hannah Walker Johnson, whose encouragement and support inspired me to press forward, and to my lovely wife Deedre, who always believed in me and who entered into this developing resource with me. I am forever grateful to Christ for the gift I have in you.

INTRODUCTION

I can see her now, vividly in my mind's eye, as she faithfully began her daily practice. As a child, I would walk slowly past her bedroom door. As I would peer through the slightly opened door, I'd watch with a deep sense of awe as the light from the early morning sun shined brightly through her bedroom windows as if to indicate the glory of God had filled the room. I'd see her sitting up in her bed as she got ready to meet with Him. Then she would sing a sweet melody from her hymnal. After she concluded singing her song to the Savior, my dear grandmother would get on her knees and pray.

You see, when my grandmother, who we affectionately called Mamita—which means "little mama" in Spanish—prayed, you knew the angels of heaven hushed their singing because God was listening. When she finished talking with God, she then sat up, opened her Bible, and read. I'd often hear her mouthing what she was reading in a soft whisper. Then she would supplement her Bible reading with her Adult Bible Study Guide. Finally, after finishing the lesson, she would get back down on her knees and talk to God in prayer.

I must have watched my grandmother do this a thousand times while I was growing up. She did this faithfully every day. She'd have her quiet time with Jesus and then begin her day. As I am writing, Mamita just passed away at 101 years old and was the godliest woman I've ever known. Her very presence just oozed with the peace and joy of Christ's presence. One thing was for sure in my young mind. My grandmother knew Jesus, and it showed!

As I've grown, I have personally discovered the love of God is compelling and beautiful as it flows forth from the pages of Scripture. Through the Scriptures, the Holy Spirit seeks to draw us to salvation by grace through faith in Jesus Christ. When one's heart is finally convicted and subdued by the drawing of the Holy Spirit, then they experience surrendering to Christ as Savior from sin, and He becomes Lord of their life. Then baptism is the public demonstration of this inward change of heart. But then what?

I remember when I got baptized at twelve years old that no one sat down with me and showed me how to grow in my daily relationship with Jesus practically. So why don't we let Jesus show us how?

CHAPTER 1
Jesus Is Our Model

Come with me into the Scriptures and see, with your mind's eye, the devotional life of Jesus. Watch Him as He rises early in the morning before the busyness of the day got started. He walks out into the quiet stillness of the early morning and finds a place of solitude to pray to His Father. The Gospel of Mark captures the scene very well. *"Now in the morning, having risen a long while before daylight, He went out and departed to a solitary place; and there He prayed"* (Mark 1:35). Jesus began His day with prayer. Before He engaged in the overwhelming demands of His day, He spent quality time with the Father.

It was in a solitary place that was more than likely a quiet location. This quiet place where Jesus often prayed to the Father was often in nature. *"And when He had sent them away, He departed to the mountain to pray"* (Mark 6:46). Again the Scriptures say, *"So He Himself often withdrew into the wilderness and prayed"* (Luke 5:16).

He not only prayed early in the morning, but He also prayed at night. He prayed with such intensity that the Bible records He once prayed all night. *"Now it came to pass in those days that He went out to the mountain to pray, and continued all night in prayer to God"* (Luke 6:12).

Those moments with His Father must have been so precious to Him. His connection with His Father was so close that His will was surrendered to and bound up with the Father's will. So much so that when He faced the most crucial moment in His life and ministry, He could present His request honestly, but still pray for His Father's will to be done. *"He went a little farther and fell on His face, and prayed, saying, 'O My Father, if it is possible, let this cup pass from Me; nevertheless, not as I will, but as You will'"* (Matthew 26:39).

Jesus' prayer time with His Father was also attractive to His followers. *"Now it came to pass, as He was praying in a certain place, when He ceased, that one of His disciples said to Him, 'Lord, teach us to pray, as John also taught his disciples'"* (Luke 11:1). Apparently, after Jesus' disciples saw Jesus pray, His disciples wanted Him to teach them how to pray as He did! However, there was something else vitally important to Jesus' devotional experience.

Jesus, from an early age, demonstrated He spent a lot of time in the Scriptures. Luke describes a scene when Jesus was just twelve years old that reveals the astonishing insights He had in the Word that can only come from Him spending time reading, studying, and meditating on it. *"Now so it was that after three days they found Him in the temple, sitting in the midst of the teachers, both listening to them and asking them questions. And all who heard Him were astonished at His understanding and answers"* (Luke 2:46-47).

Later on in His life, at the outset of His ministry, the devil came and tempted Him about His divine identity. His immediate response gives us a glimpse into how dependent He was on hearing from His Father through the Scriptures. *"Now when the tempter came to Him, he said,' If You are the Son of God, command that these stones become bread.' But He answered and said, 'It is written, "Man shall not live by bread alone, but by every word that proceeds from the mouth of God"'"* (Matthew 4:3-4).

This was not just something Jesus said. It was something He lived.

As we have journeyed through these biblical windows into the devotional life of Jesus, we are struck with two simple, yet essential ingredients to how Jesus stayed in close relationship with His Father. He maintained regular communication with His Father by talking to Him in prayer and hearing from Him through Scripture.

At the time of this writing, I have been married for over thirteen years, and I have discovered that any healthy relationship is based on regular communication and quality time. Intimacy and friendship are developed as you spend quality time with someone, listening to them, and then talking to them. When you do this on a regular basis, you begin to know this person's character, and if you like what you discover, you are likely to become intimately drawn to them.

My friend, this is what happens when we spend time with God, listening to Him speak directly to us through the Bible, and then we talk back to Him through prayer. This is what Jesus did, and since we are followers of Jesus, His love compels us to enter into the same experience.

My Experience

As I mentioned earlier, I was baptized at twelve years old. However, I must confess I didn't truly start to take knowing Jesus personally through Scripture seriously until I went to university. I had grown up knowing the truths of the Bible, reading portions of it, and reading what others said about it, but the conviction came over me one day to really know God for myself through reading the Bible. Around this time, an elder from my church gave me a Bible-reading plan in which, by the end of the year, I would have read through the entire Bible.

Initially, the thought of doing this was quite intimidating, but I decided to give it a try. It was ultimately a very deep and rewarding experience. However, I found I rushed through the experience to complete the plan because I had pride in the idea I read the entire Bible. I relished for a little while in my accomplishment and then put the Bible down. After a while, I felt the major difference not being regularly in the Bible had on my life, but I knew I didn't just want to rush through the experience again. This time, I wanted a way to do it where I was truly soaking in the Word and more intentionally growing in my relationship with Jesus.

It was several years later that the thought of journaling came to my mind. Now, growing up, I had always admired people who journaled in their devotional life with Jesus. They always seemed super spiritual to me. However, I honestly never thought I would ever get into it or be able to sustain it...until about ten years ago. And ever since I started journaling in the way I am about to show you, my life has never been the same since! I am now completely in love with Jesus. So what made the difference?

I found that intentionally journaling through the unfolding story of Scripture with a "Gospel lens" focused my thoughts in an intentional way that has major life-transforming power! What do I mean by reading the Bible with a gospel lens?

CHAPTER 2
See the Story with a Gospel Lens

The gospel can be summarized as the love of God revealed in Jesus Christ and Him crucified for our salvation and the establishment of His kingdom on Earth. The entire Bible is its epic, unfolding story. In light of this gospel lens, I'm personally inviting you to enter the story that daily leads you to Jesus by reading, meditating, and journaling through Scripture. Like a movie, this story unfolds in a series of seven scenes called

Pre-Creation, Creation, Fall, Promise, Messiah, Kingdom, and Re-Creation.

Below is a brief summary of the story…

PRE-CREATION

God existing in an eternal friendship of three co-equal Persons characterized by pure other-centered love.

CREATION

Out of this uncontainable love, God creates the universe to exist and thrive under His reign of love, with humanity perfectly reflecting His image of love on Earth as His crowning act of creation.

FALL

The angel, Lucifer, rebels against God's character and reign of love and brings the rebellion to Earth. When humanity fell by his deception, he thus usurped God's reign through humanity, on Earth, and claimed Earth as his dominion.

PROMISE

God makes the promise to redeem humanity, restore us back into His image, and reestablish His reign of love on Earth through the Messiah by making a series of unfolding covenant promises which humanity and Abraham's descendants failed to keep.

MESSIAH

Jesus arrives as the fulfillment of the covenant promises and the King, who will reestablish God's reign of love on Earth through His life, death, and resurrection. He returns to heaven to reign with the Father and minister His saving blood as our High Priest.

KINGDOM

After Christ's ascension and through the Holy Spirit, His revolutionary disciple-making movement continues to expand His kingdom on Earth. It was formed by Jesus, deformed by middle ages Papal Christianity, reformed by the Protestant movement and is presently being restored until the return of the King.

RE-CREATION

Ushered in by the second coming of Jesus and the first resurrection, all who received the gospel of the kingdom are taken to heaven to reign with Christ for 1000 years as His bride. During this time, Satan and the other fallen angels are bound to the earth in desolate misery, and the redeemed are invited to evaluate God's character in His dealings with lost humanity. This period is concluded by the second resurrection, the ending of all evil and the renewing or re-creating of the earth fully under God's reign of love forever.

Tips on Getting Started

1. **Be alert.** I've found that after I wake up, washing my face, and getting a nice cool glass of water helps prevent me from falling back asleep.
2. **Find a quiet, solitary place.** Jesus would often have a place He would go to commune with the Father. It was a quiet, solitary place. This place needs to be a place free of distraction and preferably one that inspires thought for you. For me, it has sometimes been at my desk, with a nearby view of nature outside.
3. **Bring your Bible.** This is obviously essential to this experience with Jesus. I recommend you have an easy-to-understand Bible, but also rather close to the original language. In my experience, that would be the INTERLINEAR BIBLE, NKJV, NASB, NET, or NLT versions of the Bible. Maybe you know of another. Use it.
4. **Use a highlighter.** As you read, God will reveal to you some pretty amazing things. I like to highlight them so I can come back to them and write my thoughts on them down in the journal.
5. **Have a pen.** You will need this to write your insights down in the journal.
6. **Music.** As you will soon discover, I like to begin my time with Jesus with a song. Nothing ushers you into the presence of God like a good song of worship, praise, or devotional meditation. I like to

either sing this song directly to God, or since my wife is usually still sleeping when I do this, I listen to a song. A hymnal or a song from your music library is helpful.

CHAPTER 3
How to Use This Journal

So now, let's talk practically about how to use this daily devotional journal. The first thing to know is this is about spending time with Jesus, so this needs to be the first thing you do to start your day. To really get the most out of this experience, you need to see the tangible difference this makes in the rest of your day. Also remember, we are followers of Jesus, and as we already discovered, this is how He began His day. So let's begin!

Before You Start...

Sing. Sing to God or listen to one song of praise, worship, or devotional meditation that draws you close to Him. This is great for setting the atmosphere and shifting your heart and mind toward God.

Pray. Pray a short prayer of thanksgiving that welcomes God's presence. Ask Him to reveal to you what He is like in what you read. Ask Him to give you the assurance of salvation in Jesus through what you read. Ask the Holy Spirit to speak to you through the Bible reading and give you understanding. These are some helpful and meaningful things to ask as you talk to God before you read.

Enter the Story...

Read. Read the portion of Scripture you've been given from the Bible reading plan for the day. Read at a pace that allows you to absorb what you are reading. Is what you are reading poetry, prophecy, wisdom literature, or narrative? These are just some things to think about as you read. However, there are four specific things you are looking for as you read. These are things you will want to highlight.

1. What did you see in God's character of love?
2. As the greatest revelation of God's love, what picture of Jesus or Him crucified gave you assurance of salvation?

3. In light of your assurance in Christ, what did the Holy Spirit say to you or ask you to do?
4. Based on what He said, write at least one verse you will meditate on and memorize today.

These are important because this is what you will journal about.

Meditate. After you have read the day's reading, it is really important and highly beneficial to soak in it through silent meditation. Simply close your Bible and allow your mind to be drawn into each scene again. If it is a story, allow your mind to use your senses in each scene. What do you smell, see, taste, touch, or hear? Do you identify with the experience of each character?

You are also being still in quiet reflection to listen. This is essential to learning how to discern the voice of the One who loves you and is actually speaking personally to you through the Scriptures. I have found the Scriptures call us to meditate on God's Word far more than it calls us to study it, as important as that is. So take the time to meditate after you read for as long or as short as you can as long as the experience is quality, and you have heard from God. I've personally found going for a walk outside, as close to nature as possible, takes meditating, to listen, to another level of intimacy with Jesus.

Journal. After reading and meditating, I've found one of the most powerful and life-transforming things to do is to journal based on the insights you found and highlighted in reference to the four entries. You will write them in your journal under each of these four entry statements/questions, each of which I explain below...

You're not seeking to journal exhaustively based on everything you've highlighted, but rather on that which sticks out in your mind the most from what you've highlighted and meditated on. If you want to refer back to something specific that you've highlighted, then feel free, but just be aware of the temptation to write everything you've highlighted. You may not have time to write out all the Gospel goodness you'll find!

1. **Tell God what you saw in His character of love from today's reading.** In First John 4:8-16, the Bible tells us, "God is love." This is the essence of His character. Therefore, everything we see in the Bible that describes what God is like in character is profoundly and beautifully revealing this central truth to us.

- A great example of this is in Exodus 34:5-7 when Moses asked to see the glory of God. What God does is declare His character to Moses. Here are some attributes of His character He shares with Moses: He is merciful, gracious, long-suffering, abounding in goodness, truth, He forgives, and yet doesn't clear the guilty. All of these character traits are expressions of God's love.

- I've discovered that even God's judgment and anger are expressions of His love. God is like a wounded Husband who is jealous and hurt by His wife's continual unfaithfulness. According to 2 Corinthians 3:18, it is by beholding His glory (character of love) that we become changed into the same character.

- This first journal entry is designed to help you get more intimately acquainted with what God is like. When someone is on a date, they are primarily interested in getting to know the other person. What they are like in character. Think of this time as being on a date with God every morning and allowing Him to make known to you what He is really like.

- As you write down your discoveries in this section, try to make it personal by writing, "You are…" For example, based on Exodus 34:5-7, you could write, "You are merciful, gracious, forgiving…" etc. Tell God by using "You are" (or similar phrases) to tell Him what you saw in Him personally.

- In your Bible reading, the revelation of His love will be seen in any member of the Divine Godhead; Father, Son, or Holy Spirit. Yet the greatest revelation of God's love is seen most vividly and clearly in Jesus and Him crucified for our salvation, which you will reserve for the next journal entry...

2. **As the greatest revelation of God's love, what picture of Jesus or Him crucified gave you assurance of salvation from today's reading?** Jesus taught He was the theme of all Scripture, especially what He would accomplish for our salvation on the cross. (See John 5:38-40, Luke 24:27, 32, 44-47).

- The apostle Paul felt so strongly about this that he said, "...I determined not to know anything among you except Jesus Christ and Him crucified" (1 Corinthians 2:2). It is Jesus and Him crucified that vividly provides the greatest revelation of God's love as Paul writes to the church in Rome, "But God demonstrates His own love toward us, in that while we were still sinners, Christ died for us" (Romans 5:8).

- What Jesus did for us on the cross justified us, or made us right with God, freely by grace, without any contribution on our part, which is what Paul meant when he said we were "...justified freely by His grace through the redemption that is in Christ Jesus" (Romans 3:24). It is because of this that our hearts are drawn to Jesus to confess our sin and turn from it to His grace, so we receive the present assurance of our salvation in Jesus.

- Having been made right with God through Jesus, we stand free from guilt, shame, or condemnation. Therefore, Paul says, "There is therefore *now* no condemnation to those who are in Christ Jesus, who do not walk according to the flesh, but according to the Spirit" (Romans 8:1, emphasis added). What I love most about this verse is that no matter when you come to it, it always reads "now" to remind us that right now, in Christ, we are not condemned! Having been set free from the condemnation of sin, we are free to grow in grace by the power of the Holy Spirit.

- We are not saved by our works, but rather we are saved for good works (See Ephesians 2:8-10). This wonderful good news runs like a scarlet thread from Genesis to Revelation, often in the form of pictures that reveal this central truth in Jesus. For example, in the Old Testament, the ark by which Noah, his family, and the animals were saved from the flood was a picture of Jesus and Him crucified.

- The various sacrificial offerings given to God by which the repentant sinner was accepted and forgiven was a picture of Jesus and Him crucified. Abraham offering his only beloved covenant son of promise, Isaac, as a sacrifice, but God stopping it as a test of Abraham's faith, was a stunning picture of Jesus and Him crucified. David defeating Goliath on behalf of Israel was a picture of Jesus and Him crucified. Even in the New Testament within the story of Jesus' life in the four Gospels, Jesus healing people physically by faith was a picture of Him saving us by faith through the cross. Jesus delivering people from demon possession demonstrated His power to save us from sin and Satan's power through the cross. Jesus turning water into wine as a symbol of His saving blood, Jesus feeding the 5000 with bread from heaven as a symbol of His broken body given to us as a more than satisfying gracious gift and Jesus' invitation to come to Him and find rest all vividly point to His gift of salvation accomplished for us at the cross.

- As you see this picture of Jesus and Him crucified every day in Scripture, I can tell you from personal experience, you WILL have the assurance of salvation in Him daily! It's in light of this reality that you move into the next entry...

3. **In light of your assurance in Christ, what did the Holy Spirit say to you or ask you**

to do from today's reading? This will become very clear to you after you have spent the time meditating on the reading for the day, listening for God's voice.

- The Holy Spirit will often impress your mind with key verses that particularly spoke to you from the reading and apply directly to your current life circumstances. He may also speak to you through the experience of one character you read about in a story that directly relates to your experience. The Holy Spirit will speak encouragement to you, give you instructions He intends for you to obey (apply to your life by His power), ask you to share something with someone, correct you, rebuke you, or convict you of sin in your life to lead you to grace or comfort your heart.

- Yet always remember that whatever He speaks to you, it is in light of God's love for you revealed in Jesus and Him crucified for your salvation; or in other words, what you journaled about in entries 1 and 2 …the gospel! Then write it down as though God is speaking directly to you—because He is!

4. **Based on what He said, write at least one verse from today's reading that you will meditate on and memorize today?** This

daily experience with Jesus actually comes down to just one verse. That's right, just one! Eventually, you may want to do a few more, but one verse is good for now. This one verse will be what you hide in your heart through meditation and memorization for the day.

- The Bible says, *"Your word I have hidden in my heart, that I might not sin against You"* (Psalm 119:11). The Holy Spirit actually uses this powerful practice to help you resist sin throughout the day! The Bible also says, *"I will meditate on Your precepts, and contemplate Your ways"* (119:15).

- Hiding this one verse in your heart through meditation is also a part of your contemplating the ways of the LORD, which is reflecting on His character of love. This is why the Holy Spirit uses this to help you resist the temptation to sin we all have during the day because your heart will be abiding in the love of God. Yes, you will have an amazing experience with Jesus journaling through Scripture to start your day, but the truth is it doesn't take very long in the day for us to realize just how much we desperately need Him again! Therefore, I encourage you to maintain a conversation with Him throughout the day in prayer over the big or small things of life, which is like oxygen to the soul.

- Yet, I equally encourage you to select just one verse from the reading, usually coming from one key verse the Holy Spirit impressed on your mind while meditating on what He said to you that day (entry 3) to help you re-center back on abiding in Jesus at critical moments in your day. This is such a beautiful experience that I do not want you to miss the power of this!

- It's actually quite simple. Just take at least five minutes at three different times in your day, which will likely be sometime around when you eat breakfast, lunch, and dinner. In this moment, it's good to relax your body as much as possible, be still, breathe slowly and deeply, and then meditate on your verse. Say the verse slowly seven times, beginning and ending the verse with the Scripture reference (ex: Psalm 119:11) each time. It's like a sandwich: Scripture reference + verse + Scripture reference. Each time you say the verse, it's good to pause and reflect on the meaning, imagery, or application of the verse to your life. Briefly meditating on this one verse also has a trigger effect that brings back to your memory the larger context of the Scripture portion you read and journaled about that morning from which you got this verse.

LIFE IN CHRIST

Recommended Outline for Closing Pray

1. Thank God for at least one attribute of **His character of love** you saw in today's reading.
2. Go to the cross, confess any known sin, and accept, by faith, God's forgiveness in light of the picture of **Jesus and Him Crucified** you saw in today's reading.
3. Pray for the baptism of **the Holy Spirit**. Ask Him to give you an opportunity to share Jesus today.
4. Pray for others' needs.
5. Pray for your personal needs.
6. Close by thanking Him, surrender requests to His will, In Jesus' name.

Enter the Story Together

This daily devotional journal is intentionally designed to lead to discussion in a weekly small group gathering with others you invite to take this journey with you. As a matter of fact, start praying now for the Holy Spirit to lead you to three people in the places and spaces where you do life (at home, work, school, church, neighborhood, etc.) to take this journey with you.

The conversation you will have each week will be based on the journal entries you all would have already written down during the week. Here's what a weekly sample gathering and discussion questions would look like (time of gathering will vary):

5:00 pm - Refreshments & Conversation
5:10 pm - Discuss Devotional Journal Entries

1. Share at least one aspect of **God's character of love** that stood out to you this week.
2. Share at least one picture of **Jesus or Him crucified** that gave you assurance of salvation this week.
3. Share at least one thing **the Holy Spirit said** to you or asked you to do this week. How can we pray for you in your obedience to the Spirit?
4. Can you share at least **one verse** you meditated on from memory?

5. Can you give an update on the **three people** you're praying for to take this journey with you? How can we pray for them?

6:10 pm - **Pray Together**
6:20 pm - **Announcements and End**

CONCLUSION

Encouragement for the Journey

As you get ready to take this life-transforming journey, I just want to encourage you as you get started. In light of Christ's overwhelming love and commitment to a relationship with you, I sincerely pray you will enter into this experience from a heart of gratitude for His abundant grace, in love for Him, and in commitment to Him.

After reading this instructional guide, you might possibly feel like this may be a lot for each day. Rest assured, it is not. I took the time to explain this daily rhythm in Christ with you to give you a solid place from which to launch into this experience with Him. But as you will see in the daily devotional journal template on the next page, it's actually quite simple, and remember, it all whittles down to a single verse you will hide in your heart each day.

We wanted to make this resource more accessible and have therefore designed it to be used with any Bible reading plan that suites your current stage of spiritual development. For example you may do a 30-day reading plan all the way up to a full 365-day reading plan, thus this daily devotional journal goes up to 365 days. Thus, we've made several Bible reading plans available for you to "Enter the Story" each day with this journal at http://livingforhim.tv. When you visit our website, click on "Equipping" to find the Enter the Story reading plan that's just for you, whether a book of the Bible, The New Testament in a year, The Old & New Testament in a year, or the Chronological plan in a year. This daily devotional journal may also be used with any other Bible reading plans. We especially recommend the ones found on the YouVersion Bible app. We'd love to hear how this resource is being a blessing to you, so please email us at info@livingforhim.tv. Our prayer is that you experience the joy of life in Christ!

Date: _____ Song: _____ Today's Scripture: _____

1. Tell God what you saw in His character of love.

   _____
   _____
   _____
   _____

2. As the greatest revelation of God's love, what picture of Jesus or Him crucified gave you the assurance of salvation today?

   _____
   _____
   _____
   _____

3. In light of your assurance in Christ, what did the Holy Spirit say to you or ask you to do?

   _____
   _____
   _____
   _____

4. Based on what He said, write at least one verse you will meditate on and memorize today?

   _____
   _____
   _____
   _____

Date: _____ Song: _____ Today's Scripture: _____

1. Tell God what you saw in His character of love.

   _____
   _____
   _____
   _____

2. As the greatest revelation of God's love, what picture of Jesus or Him crucified gave you the assurance of salvation today?

   _____
   _____
   _____
   _____

3. In light of your assurance in Christ, what did the Holy Spirit say to you or ask you to do?

   _____
   _____
   _____
   _____

4. Based on what He said, write at least one verse you will meditate on and memorize today?

   _____
   _____
   _____
   _____

Date: _____ Song: _____ Today's Scripture: _____

1. Tell God what you saw in His character of love.

   _____
   _____
   _____
   _____

2. As the greatest revelation of God's love, what picture of Jesus or Him crucified gave you the assurance of salvation today?

   _____
   _____
   _____
   _____

3. In light of your assurance in Christ, what did the Holy Spirit say to you or ask you to do?

   _____
   _____
   _____
   _____

4. Based on what He said, write at least one verse you will meditate on and memorize today?

   _____
   _____
   _____
   _____

Date: _____ Song: _____ Today's Scripture: _____

1. Tell God what you saw in His character of love.
   _____
   _____
   _____
   _____

2. As the greatest revelation of God's love, what picture of Jesus or Him crucified gave you the assurance of salvation today?
   _____
   _____
   _____
   _____

3. In light of your assurance in Christ, what did the Holy Spirit say to you or ask you to do?
   _____
   _____
   _____
   _____

4. Based on what He said, write at least one verse you will meditate on and memorize today?
   _____
   _____
   _____
   _____

Date: _____ Song: _____ Today's Scripture: _____

1. Tell God what you saw in His character of love.

   _____
   _____
   _____
   _____

2. As the greatest revelation of God's love, what picture of Jesus or Him crucified gave you the assurance of salvation today?

   _____
   _____
   _____
   _____

3. In light of your assurance in Christ, what did the Holy Spirit say to you or ask you to do?

   _____
   _____
   _____
   _____

4. Based on what He said, write at least one verse you will meditate on and memorize today?

   _____
   _____
   _____
   _____

Date: _____ Song: _____ Today's Scripture: _____

1. Tell God what you saw in His character of love.
   _____
   _____
   _____
   _____

2. As the greatest revelation of God's love, what picture of Jesus or Him crucified gave you the assurance of salvation today?
   _____
   _____
   _____
   _____

3. In light of your assurance in Christ, what did the Holy Spirit say to you or ask you to do?
   _____
   _____
   _____
   _____

4. Based on what He said, write at least one verse you will meditate on and memorize today?
   _____
   _____
   _____
   _____

Date: _____ Song: _____ Today's Scripture: _____

1. Tell God what you saw in His character of love.

   _____
   _____
   _____
   _____

2. As the greatest revelation of God's love, what picture of Jesus or Him crucified gave you the assurance of salvation today?

   _____
   _____
   _____
   _____

3. In light of your assurance in Christ, what did the Holy Spirit say to you or ask you to do?

   _____
   _____
   _____
   _____

4. Based on what He said, write at least one verse you will meditate on and memorize today?

   _____
   _____
   _____
   _____

Date: _____ Song: _____ Today's Scripture: _____

1. Tell God what you saw in His character of love.
   _____
   _____
   _____
   _____

2. As the greatest revelation of God's love, what picture of Jesus or Him crucified gave you the assurance of salvation today?
   _____
   _____
   _____
   _____

3. In light of your assurance in Christ, what did the Holy Spirit say to you or ask you to do?
   _____
   _____
   _____
   _____

4. Based on what He said, write at least one verse you will meditate on and memorize today?
   _____
   _____
   _____
   _____

Date: _____ Song: _____ Today's Scripture: _____

1. Tell God what you saw in His character of love.

   _____
   _____
   _____
   _____

2. As the greatest revelation of God's love, what picture of Jesus or Him crucified gave you the assurance of salvation today?

   _____
   _____
   _____
   _____

3. In light of your assurance in Christ, what did the Holy Spirit say to you or ask you to do?

   _____
   _____
   _____
   _____

4. Based on what He said, write at least one verse you will meditate on and memorize today?

   _____
   _____
   _____
   _____

Date: _____ Song: _____ Today's Scripture: _____

1. Tell God what you saw in His character of love.
   _____
   _____
   _____
   _____

2. As the greatest revelation of God's love, what picture of Jesus or Him crucified gave you the assurance of salvation today?
   _____
   _____
   _____
   _____

3. In light of your assurance in Christ, what did the Holy Spirit say to you or ask you to do?
   _____
   _____
   _____
   _____

4. Based on what He said, write at least one verse you will meditate on and memorize today?
   _____
   _____
   _____
   _____

Date: _____ Song: _____ Today's Scripture: _____

1. Tell God what you saw in His character of love.

   _____
   _____
   _____
   _____

2. As the greatest revelation of God's love, what picture of Jesus or Him crucified gave you the assurance of salvation today?

   _____
   _____
   _____
   _____

3. In light of your assurance in Christ, what did the Holy Spirit say to you or ask you to do?

   _____
   _____
   _____
   _____

4. Based on what He said, write at least one verse you will meditate on and memorize today?

   _____
   _____
   _____
   _____

Date: _____ Song: _____ Today's Scripture: _____

1. Tell God what you saw in His character of love.

   _____
   _____
   _____
   _____

2. As the greatest revelation of God's love, what picture of Jesus or Him crucified gave you the assurance of salvation today?

   _____
   _____
   _____
   _____

3. In light of your assurance in Christ, what did the Holy Spirit say to you or ask you to do?

   _____
   _____
   _____
   _____

4. Based on what He said, write at least one verse you will meditate on and memorize today?

   _____
   _____
   _____
   _____

Date: _____ Song: _____ Today's Scripture: _____

1. Tell God what you saw in His character of love.

   _____
   _____
   _____
   _____

2. As the greatest revelation of God's love, what picture of Jesus or Him crucified gave you the assurance of salvation today?

   _____
   _____
   _____
   _____

3. In light of your assurance in Christ, what did the Holy Spirit say to you or ask you to do?

   _____
   _____
   _____
   _____

4. Based on what He said, write at least one verse you will meditate on and memorize today?

   _____
   _____
   _____
   _____

Date: _____ Song: _____ Today's Scripture: _____

1. Tell God what you saw in His character of love.
   _____
   _____
   _____
   _____

2. As the greatest revelation of God's love, what picture of Jesus or Him crucified gave you the assurance of salvation today?
   _____
   _____
   _____
   _____

3. In light of your assurance in Christ, what did the Holy Spirit say to you or ask you to do?
   _____
   _____
   _____
   _____

4. Based on what He said, write at least one verse you will meditate on and memorize today?
   _____
   _____
   _____
   _____

Date: _____ Song: _____ Today's Scripture: _____

1. Tell God what you saw in His character of love.

   _____
   _____
   _____
   _____

2. As the greatest revelation of God's love, what picture of Jesus or Him crucified gave you the assurance of salvation today?

   _____
   _____
   _____
   _____

3. In light of your assurance in Christ, what did the Holy Spirit say to you or ask you to do?

   _____
   _____
   _____
   _____

4. Based on what He said, write at least one verse you will meditate on and memorize today?

   _____
   _____
   _____
   _____

Date: _____ Song: _____ Today's Scripture: _____

1. Tell God what you saw in His character of love.
   _____
   _____
   _____
   _____

2. As the greatest revelation of God's love, what picture of Jesus or Him crucified gave you the assurance of salvation today?
   _____
   _____
   _____
   _____

3. In light of your assurance in Christ, what did the Holy Spirit say to you or ask you to do?
   _____
   _____
   _____
   _____

4. Based on what He said, write at least one verse you will meditate on and memorize today?
   _____
   _____
   _____
   _____

Date: _____ Song: _____ Today's Scripture: _____

1. Tell God what you saw in His character of love.

   _____
   _____
   _____
   _____

2. As the greatest revelation of God's love, what picture of Jesus or Him crucified gave you the assurance of salvation today?

   _____
   _____
   _____
   _____

3. In light of your assurance in Christ, what did the Holy Spirit say to you or ask you to do?

   _____
   _____
   _____
   _____

4. Based on what He said, write at least one verse you will meditate on and memorize today?

   _____
   _____
   _____
   _____

Date: _____ Song: _____ Today's Scripture: _____

1. Tell God what you saw in His character of love.

   _____
   _____
   _____
   _____

2. As the greatest revelation of God's love, what picture of Jesus or Him crucified gave you the assurance of salvation today?

   _____
   _____
   _____
   _____

3. In light of your assurance in Christ, what did the Holy Spirit say to you or ask you to do?

   _____
   _____
   _____
   _____

4. Based on what He said, write at least one verse you will meditate on and memorize today?

   _____
   _____
   _____
   _____

Date: _____ Song: _____ Today's Scripture: _____

1. Tell God what you saw in His character of love.

   _____
   _____
   _____
   _____

2. As the greatest revelation of God's love, what picture of Jesus or Him crucified gave you the assurance of salvation today?

   _____
   _____
   _____
   _____

3. In light of your assurance in Christ, what did the Holy Spirit say to you or ask you to do?

   _____
   _____
   _____
   _____

4. Based on what He said, write at least one verse you will meditate on and memorize today?

   _____
   _____
   _____
   _____

Date: _____ Song: _____ Today's Scripture: _____

1. Tell God what you saw in His character of love.

   _____
   _____
   _____
   _____

2. As the greatest revelation of God's love, what picture of Jesus or Him crucified gave you the assurance of salvation today?

   _____
   _____
   _____
   _____

3. In light of your assurance in Christ, what did the Holy Spirit say to you or ask you to do?

   _____
   _____
   _____
   _____

4. Based on what He said, write at least one verse you will meditate on and memorize today?

   _____
   _____
   _____
   _____

Date: _____ Song: _____ Today's Scripture: _____

1. Tell God what you saw in His character of love.

   _____
   _____
   _____
   _____

2. As the greatest revelation of God's love, what picture of Jesus or Him crucified gave you the assurance of salvation today?

   _____
   _____
   _____
   _____

3. In light of your assurance in Christ, what did the Holy Spirit say to you or ask you to do?

   _____
   _____
   _____
   _____

4. Based on what He said, write at least one verse you will meditate on and memorize today?

   _____
   _____
   _____
   _____

Date: _____ Song: _____ Today's Scripture: _____

1. Tell God what you saw in His character of love.

   _____
   _____
   _____
   _____

2. As the greatest revelation of God's love, what picture of Jesus or Him crucified gave you the assurance of salvation today?

   _____
   _____
   _____
   _____

3. In light of your assurance in Christ, what did the Holy Spirit say to you or ask you to do?

   _____
   _____
   _____
   _____

4. Based on what He said, write at least one verse you will meditate on and memorize today?

   _____
   _____
   _____
   _____

Date: _____ Song: _____ Today's Scripture: _____

1. Tell God what you saw in His character of love.

   _____
   _____
   _____
   _____

2. As the greatest revelation of God's love, what picture of Jesus or Him crucified gave you the assurance of salvation today?

   _____
   _____
   _____
   _____

3. In light of your assurance in Christ, what did the Holy Spirit say to you or ask you to do?

   _____
   _____
   _____
   _____

4. Based on what He said, write at least one verse you will meditate on and memorize today?

   _____
   _____
   _____
   _____

Date: _____ Song: _____ Today's Scripture: _____

1. Tell God what you saw in His character of love.
   _____
   _____
   _____
   _____

2. As the greatest revelation of God's love, what picture of Jesus or Him crucified gave you the assurance of salvation today?
   _____
   _____
   _____
   _____

3. In light of your assurance in Christ, what did the Holy Spirit say to you or ask you to do?
   _____
   _____
   _____
   _____

4. Based on what He said, write at least one verse you will meditate on and memorize today?
   _____
   _____
   _____
   _____

Date: _____ Song: _____ Today's Scripture: _____

1. Tell God what you saw in His character of love.

   _____
   _____
   _____
   _____

2. As the greatest revelation of God's love, what picture of Jesus or Him crucified gave you the assurance of salvation today?

   _____
   _____
   _____
   _____

3. In light of your assurance in Christ, what did the Holy Spirit say to you or ask you to do?

   _____
   _____
   _____
   _____

4. Based on what He said, write at least one verse you will meditate on and memorize today?

   _____
   _____
   _____
   _____

Date: _____ Song: _____ Today's Scripture: _____

1. Tell God what you saw in His character of love.

   _____
   _____
   _____
   _____

2. As the greatest revelation of God's love, what picture of Jesus or Him crucified gave you the assurance of salvation today?

   _____
   _____
   _____
   _____

3. In light of your assurance in Christ, what did the Holy Spirit say to you or ask you to do?

   _____
   _____
   _____
   _____

4. Based on what He said, write at least one verse you will meditate on and memorize today?

   _____
   _____
   _____
   _____

Date: _____ Song: _____ Today's Scripture: _____

1. Tell God what you saw in His character of love.

   _____
   _____
   _____
   _____

2. As the greatest revelation of God's love, what picture of Jesus or Him crucified gave you the assurance of salvation today?

   _____
   _____
   _____
   _____

3. In light of your assurance in Christ, what did the Holy Spirit say to you or ask you to do?

   _____
   _____
   _____
   _____

4. Based on what He said, write at least one verse you will meditate on and memorize today?

   _____
   _____
   _____
   _____

Date: _____ Song: _____ Today's Scripture: _____

1. Tell God what you saw in His character of love.
   _____
   _____
   _____
   _____

2. As the greatest revelation of God's love, what picture of Jesus or Him crucified gave you the assurance of salvation today?
   _____
   _____
   _____
   _____

3. In light of your assurance in Christ, what did the Holy Spirit say to you or ask you to do?
   _____
   _____
   _____
   _____

4. Based on what He said, write at least one verse you will meditate on and memorize today?
   _____
   _____
   _____
   _____

Date: _____ Song: _____ Today's Scripture: _____

1. Tell God what you saw in His character of love.

   _____
   _____
   _____
   _____

2. As the greatest revelation of God's love, what picture of Jesus or Him crucified gave you the assurance of salvation today?

   _____
   _____
   _____
   _____

3. In light of your assurance in Christ, what did the Holy Spirit say to you or ask you to do?

   _____
   _____
   _____
   _____

4. Based on what He said, write at least one verse you will meditate on and memorize today?

   _____
   _____
   _____
   _____

Date: _____ Song: _____ Today's Scripture: _____

1. Tell God what you saw in His character of love.

   _____
   _____
   _____
   _____

2. As the greatest revelation of God's love, what picture of Jesus or Him crucified gave you the assurance of salvation today?

   _____
   _____
   _____
   _____

3. In light of your assurance in Christ, what did the Holy Spirit say to you or ask you to do?

   _____
   _____
   _____
   _____

4. Based on what He said, write at least one verse you will meditate on and memorize today?

   _____
   _____
   _____
   _____

Date: _____ Song: _____ Today's Scripture: _____

1. Tell God what you saw in His character of love.

   _____
   _____
   _____
   _____

2. As the greatest revelation of God's love, what picture of Jesus or Him crucified gave you the assurance of salvation today?

   _____
   _____
   _____
   _____

3. In light of your assurance in Christ, what did the Holy Spirit say to you or ask you to do?

   _____
   _____
   _____
   _____

4. Based on what He said, write at least one verse you will meditate on and memorize today?

   _____
   _____
   _____
   _____

Date: _____ Song: _____ Today's Scripture: _____

1. Tell God what you saw in His character of love.
   _____
   _____
   _____
   _____

2. As the greatest revelation of God's love, what picture of Jesus or Him crucified gave you the assurance of salvation today?
   _____
   _____
   _____
   _____

3. In light of your assurance in Christ, what did the Holy Spirit say to you or ask you to do?
   _____
   _____
   _____
   _____

4. Based on what He said, write at least one verse you will meditate on and memorize today?
   _____
   _____
   _____
   _____

Date: _____ Song: _____ Today's Scripture: _____

1. Tell God what you saw in His character of love.

   _____
   _____
   _____
   _____

2. As the greatest revelation of God's love, what picture of Jesus or Him crucified gave you the assurance of salvation today?

   _____
   _____
   _____
   _____

3. In light of your assurance in Christ, what did the Holy Spirit say to you or ask you to do?

   _____
   _____
   _____
   _____

4. Based on what He said, write at least one verse you will meditate on and memorize today?

   _____
   _____
   _____
   _____

Date: _____ Song: _____ Today's Scripture: _____

1. Tell God what you saw in His character of love.
   _____
   _____
   _____
   _____

2. As the greatest revelation of God's love, what picture of Jesus or Him crucified gave you the assurance of salvation today?
   _____
   _____
   _____
   _____

3. In light of your assurance in Christ, what did the Holy Spirit say to you or ask you to do?
   _____
   _____
   _____
   _____

4. Based on what He said, write at least one verse you will meditate on and memorize today?
   _____
   _____
   _____
   _____

Date: _____ Song: _____ Today's Scripture: _____

1. Tell God what you saw in His character of love.

   _____
   _____
   _____
   _____

2. As the greatest revelation of God's love, what picture of Jesus or Him crucified gave you the assurance of salvation today?

   _____
   _____
   _____
   _____

3. In light of your assurance in Christ, what did the Holy Spirit say to you or ask you to do?

   _____
   _____
   _____
   _____

4. Based on what He said, write at least one verse you will meditate on and memorize today?

   _____
   _____
   _____
   _____

Date: _____ Song: _____ Today's Scripture: _____

1. Tell God what you saw in His character of love.

   _____
   _____
   _____
   _____

2. As the greatest revelation of God's love, what picture of Jesus or Him crucified gave you the assurance of salvation today?

   _____
   _____
   _____
   _____

3. In light of your assurance in Christ, what did the Holy Spirit say to you or ask you to do?

   _____
   _____
   _____
   _____

4. Based on what He said, write at least one verse you will meditate on and memorize today?

   _____
   _____
   _____
   _____

Date: _____ Song: _____ Today's Scripture: _____

1. Tell God what you saw in His character of love.

   _____
   _____
   _____
   _____

2. As the greatest revelation of God's love, what picture of Jesus or Him crucified gave you the assurance of salvation today?

   _____
   _____
   _____
   _____

3. In light of your assurance in Christ, what did the Holy Spirit say to you or ask you to do?

   _____
   _____
   _____
   _____

4. Based on what He said, write at least one verse you will meditate on and memorize today?

   _____
   _____
   _____
   _____

Date: _____ Song: _____ Today's Scripture: _____

1. Tell God what you saw in His character of love.
   _____
   _____
   _____
   _____

2. As the greatest revelation of God's love, what picture of Jesus or Him crucified gave you the assurance of salvation today?
   _____
   _____
   _____
   _____

3. In light of your assurance in Christ, what did the Holy Spirit say to you or ask you to do?
   _____
   _____
   _____
   _____

4. Based on what He said, write at least one verse you will meditate on and memorize today?
   _____
   _____
   _____
   _____

Date: _____ Song: _____ Today's Scripture: _____

1. Tell God what you saw in His character of love.

   _____
   _____
   _____
   _____

2. As the greatest revelation of God's love, what picture of Jesus or Him crucified gave you the assurance of salvation today?

   _____
   _____
   _____
   _____

3. In light of your assurance in Christ, what did the Holy Spirit say to you or ask you to do?

   _____
   _____
   _____
   _____

4. Based on what He said, write at least one verse you will meditate on and memorize today?

   _____
   _____
   _____
   _____

Date: _____ Song: _____ Today's Scripture: _____

1. Tell God what you saw in His character of love.

   _____
   _____
   _____
   _____

2. As the greatest revelation of God's love, what picture of Jesus or Him crucified gave you the assurance of salvation today?

   _____
   _____
   _____
   _____

3. In light of your assurance in Christ, what did the Holy Spirit say to you or ask you to do?

   _____
   _____
   _____
   _____

4. Based on what He said, write at least one verse you will meditate on and memorize today?

   _____
   _____
   _____
   _____

Date: _____ Song: _____ Today's Scripture: _____

1. Tell God what you saw in His character of love.

   _____
   _____
   _____
   _____

2. As the greatest revelation of God's love, what picture of Jesus or Him crucified gave you the assurance of salvation today?

   _____
   _____
   _____
   _____

3. In light of your assurance in Christ, what did the Holy Spirit say to you or ask you to do?

   _____
   _____
   _____
   _____

4. Based on what He said, write at least one verse you will meditate on and memorize today?

   _____
   _____
   _____
   _____

Date: _____ Song: _____ Today's Scripture: _____

1. Tell God what you saw in His character of love.
   _____
   _____
   _____
   _____

2. As the greatest revelation of God's love, what picture of Jesus or Him crucified gave you the assurance of salvation today?
   _____
   _____
   _____
   _____

3. In light of your assurance in Christ, what did the Holy Spirit say to you or ask you to do?
   _____
   _____
   _____
   _____

4. Based on what He said, write at least one verse you will meditate on and memorize today?
   _____
   _____
   _____
   _____

Date: _____ Song: _____ Today's Scripture: _____

1. Tell God what you saw in His character of love.

   _____
   _____
   _____
   _____

2. As the greatest revelation of God's love, what picture of Jesus or Him crucified gave you the assurance of salvation today?

   _____
   _____
   _____
   _____

3. In light of your assurance in Christ, what did the Holy Spirit say to you or ask you to do?

   _____
   _____
   _____
   _____

4. Based on what He said, write at least one verse you will meditate on and memorize today?

   _____
   _____
   _____
   _____

Date: _____ Song: _____ Today's Scripture: _____

1. Tell God what you saw in His character of love.
   _____
   _____
   _____
   _____

2. As the greatest revelation of God's love, what picture of Jesus or Him crucified gave you the assurance of salvation today?
   _____
   _____
   _____
   _____

3. In light of your assurance in Christ, what did the Holy Spirit say to you or ask you to do?
   _____
   _____
   _____
   _____

4. Based on what He said, write at least one verse you will meditate on and memorize today?
   _____
   _____
   _____
   _____

Date: _____ Song: _____ Today's Scripture: _____

1. Tell God what you saw in His character of love.

   _____
   _____
   _____
   _____

2. As the greatest revelation of God's love, what picture of Jesus or Him crucified gave you the assurance of salvation today?

   _____
   _____
   _____
   _____

3. In light of your assurance in Christ, what did the Holy Spirit say to you or ask you to do?

   _____
   _____
   _____
   _____

4. Based on what He said, write at least one verse you will meditate on and memorize today?

   _____
   _____
   _____
   _____

Date: _____ Song: _____ Today's Scripture: _____

1. Tell God what you saw in His character of love.

   _____
   _____
   _____
   _____

2. As the greatest revelation of God's love, what picture of Jesus or Him crucified gave you the assurance of salvation today?

   _____
   _____
   _____
   _____

3. In light of your assurance in Christ, what did the Holy Spirit say to you or ask you to do?

   _____
   _____
   _____
   _____

4. Based on what He said, write at least one verse you will meditate on and memorize today?

   _____
   _____
   _____
   _____

Date: _____ Song: _____ Today's Scripture: _____

1. Tell God what you saw in His character of love.

   _____
   _____
   _____
   _____

2. As the greatest revelation of God's love, what picture of Jesus or Him crucified gave you the assurance of salvation today?

   _____
   _____
   _____
   _____

3. In light of your assurance in Christ, what did the Holy Spirit say to you or ask you to do?

   _____
   _____
   _____
   _____

4. Based on what He said, write at least one verse you will meditate on and memorize today?

   _____
   _____
   _____
   _____

Date: _____ Song: _____ Today's Scripture: _____

1. Tell God what you saw in His character of love.
   _____
   _____
   _____
   _____

2. As the greatest revelation of God's love, what picture of Jesus or Him crucified gave you the assurance of salvation today?
   _____
   _____
   _____
   _____

3. In light of your assurance in Christ, what did the Holy Spirit say to you or ask you to do?
   _____
   _____
   _____
   _____

4. Based on what He said, write at least one verse you will meditate on and memorize today?
   _____
   _____
   _____
   _____

Date: _____ Song: _____ Today's Scripture: _____

1. Tell God what you saw in His character of love.

   _____
   _____
   _____
   _____

2. As the greatest revelation of God's love, what picture of Jesus or Him crucified gave you the assurance of salvation today?

   _____
   _____
   _____
   _____

3. In light of your assurance in Christ, what did the Holy Spirit say to you or ask you to do?

   _____
   _____
   _____
   _____

4. Based on what He said, write at least one verse you will meditate on and memorize today?

   _____
   _____
   _____
   _____

Date: _____ Song: _____ Today's Scripture: _____

1. Tell God what you saw in His character of love.

   _____
   _____
   _____
   _____

2. As the greatest revelation of God's love, what picture of Jesus or Him crucified gave you the assurance of salvation today?

   _____
   _____
   _____
   _____

3. In light of your assurance in Christ, what did the Holy Spirit say to you or ask you to do?

   _____
   _____
   _____
   _____

4. Based on what He said, write at least one verse you will meditate on and memorize today?

   _____
   _____
   _____
   _____

Date: _____ Song: _____ Today's Scripture: _____

1. Tell God what you saw in His character of love.

   _____
   _____
   _____
   _____

2. As the greatest revelation of God's love, what picture of Jesus or Him crucified gave you the assurance of salvation today?

   _____
   _____
   _____
   _____

3. In light of your assurance in Christ, what did the Holy Spirit say to you or ask you to do?

   _____
   _____
   _____
   _____

4. Based on what He said, write at least one verse you will meditate on and memorize today?

   _____
   _____
   _____
   _____

Date: _____ Song: _____ Today's Scripture: _____

1. Tell God what you saw in His character of love.
   _____
   _____
   _____
   _____

2. As the greatest revelation of God's love, what picture of Jesus or Him crucified gave you the assurance of salvation today?
   _____
   _____
   _____
   _____

3. In light of your assurance in Christ, what did the Holy Spirit say to you or ask you to do?
   _____
   _____
   _____
   _____

4. Based on what He said, write at least one verse you will meditate on and memorize today?
   _____
   _____
   _____
   _____

Date: _____ Song: _____ Today's Scripture: _____

1. Tell God what you saw in His character of love.

   _____
   _____
   _____
   _____

2. As the greatest revelation of God's love, what picture of Jesus or Him crucified gave you the assurance of salvation today?

   _____
   _____
   _____
   _____

3. In light of your assurance in Christ, what did the Holy Spirit say to you or ask you to do?

   _____
   _____
   _____
   _____

4. Based on what He said, write at least one verse you will meditate on and memorize today?

   _____
   _____
   _____
   _____

Date: _____ Song: _____ Today's Scripture: _____

1. Tell God what you saw in His character of love.
   _____
   _____
   _____
   _____

2. As the greatest revelation of God's love, what picture of Jesus or Him crucified gave you the assurance of salvation today?
   _____
   _____
   _____
   _____

3. In light of your assurance in Christ, what did the Holy Spirit say to you or ask you to do?
   _____
   _____
   _____
   _____

4. Based on what He said, write at least one verse you will meditate on and memorize today?
   _____
   _____
   _____
   _____

Date: _____ Song: _____ Today's Scripture: _____

1. Tell God what you saw in His character of love.

   _____
   _____
   _____
   _____

2. As the greatest revelation of God's love, what picture of Jesus or Him crucified gave you the assurance of salvation today?

   _____
   _____
   _____
   _____

3. In light of your assurance in Christ, what did the Holy Spirit say to you or ask you to do?

   _____
   _____
   _____
   _____

4. Based on what He said, write at least one verse you will meditate on and memorize today?

   _____
   _____
   _____
   _____

Date: _____ Song: _____ Today's Scripture: _____

1. Tell God what you saw in His character of love.
   _____
   _____
   _____
   _____

2. As the greatest revelation of God's love, what picture of Jesus or Him crucified gave you the assurance of salvation today?
   _____
   _____
   _____
   _____

3. In light of your assurance in Christ, what did the Holy Spirit say to you or ask you to do?
   _____
   _____
   _____
   _____

4. Based on what He said, write at least one verse you will meditate on and memorize today?
   _____
   _____
   _____
   _____

Date: _____ Song: _____ Today's Scripture: _____

1. Tell God what you saw in His character of love.

   _____
   _____
   _____
   _____

2. As the greatest revelation of God's love, what picture of Jesus or Him crucified gave you the assurance of salvation today?

   _____
   _____
   _____
   _____

3. In light of your assurance in Christ, what did the Holy Spirit say to you or ask you to do?

   _____
   _____
   _____
   _____

4. Based on what He said, write at least one verse you will meditate on and memorize today?

   _____
   _____
   _____
   _____

Date: _____ Song: _____ Today's Scripture: _____

1. Tell God what you saw in His character of love.
   _____
   _____
   _____
   _____

2. As the greatest revelation of God's love, what picture of Jesus or Him crucified gave you the assurance of salvation today?
   _____
   _____
   _____
   _____

3. In light of your assurance in Christ, what did the Holy Spirit say to you or ask you to do?
   _____
   _____
   _____
   _____

4. Based on what He said, write at least one verse you will meditate on and memorize today?
   _____
   _____
   _____
   _____

Date: _____ Song: _____ Today's Scripture: _____

1. Tell God what you saw in His character of love.

   _____
   _____
   _____
   _____

2. As the greatest revelation of God's love, what picture of Jesus or Him crucified gave you the assurance of salvation today?

   _____
   _____
   _____
   _____

3. In light of your assurance in Christ, what did the Holy Spirit say to you or ask you to do?

   _____
   _____
   _____
   _____

4. Based on what He said, write at least one verse you will meditate on and memorize today?

   _____
   _____
   _____
   _____

Date: _____ Song: _____ Today's Scripture: _____

1. Tell God what you saw in His character of love.
   _____
   _____
   _____
   _____

2. As the greatest revelation of God's love, what picture of Jesus or Him crucified gave you the assurance of salvation today?
   _____
   _____
   _____
   _____

3. In light of your assurance in Christ, what did the Holy Spirit say to you or ask you to do?
   _____
   _____
   _____
   _____

4. Based on what He said, write at least one verse you will meditate on and memorize today?
   _____
   _____
   _____
   _____

Date: _____ Song: _____ Today's Scripture: _____

1. Tell God what you saw in His character of love.

   _____
   _____
   _____
   _____

2. As the greatest revelation of God's love, what picture of Jesus or Him crucified gave you the assurance of salvation today?

   _____
   _____
   _____
   _____

3. In light of your assurance in Christ, what did the Holy Spirit say to you or ask you to do?

   _____
   _____
   _____
   _____

4. Based on what He said, write at least one verse you will meditate on and memorize today?

   _____
   _____
   _____
   _____

Date: _____ Song: _____ Today's Scripture: _____

1. Tell God what you saw in His character of love.

   _____
   _____
   _____
   _____

2. As the greatest revelation of God's love, what picture of Jesus or Him crucified gave you the assurance of salvation today?

   _____
   _____
   _____
   _____

3. In light of your assurance in Christ, what did the Holy Spirit say to you or ask you to do?

   _____
   _____
   _____
   _____

4. Based on what He said, write at least one verse you will meditate on and memorize today?

   _____
   _____
   _____
   _____

Date: _____ Song: _____ Today's Scripture: _____

1. Tell God what you saw in His character of love.

   _____
   _____
   _____
   _____

2. As the greatest revelation of God's love, what picture of Jesus or Him crucified gave you the assurance of salvation today?

   _____
   _____
   _____
   _____

3. In light of your assurance in Christ, what did the Holy Spirit say to you or ask you to do?

   _____
   _____
   _____
   _____

4. Based on what He said, write at least one verse you will meditate on and memorize today?

   _____
   _____
   _____
   _____

Date: _____ Song: _____ Today's Scripture: _____

1. Tell God what you saw in His character of love.

   _____
   _____
   _____
   _____

2. As the greatest revelation of God's love, what picture of Jesus or Him crucified gave you the assurance of salvation today?

   _____
   _____
   _____
   _____

3. In light of your assurance in Christ, what did the Holy Spirit say to you or ask you to do?

   _____
   _____
   _____
   _____

4. Based on what He said, write at least one verse you will meditate on and memorize today?

   _____
   _____
   _____
   _____

Date: _____ Song: _____ Today's Scripture: _____

1. Tell God what you saw in His character of love.

   _____
   _____
   _____
   _____

2. As the greatest revelation of God's love, what picture of Jesus or Him crucified gave you the assurance of salvation today?

   _____
   _____
   _____
   _____

3. In light of your assurance in Christ, what did the Holy Spirit say to you or ask you to do?

   _____
   _____
   _____
   _____

4. Based on what He said, write at least one verse you will meditate on and memorize today?

   _____
   _____
   _____
   _____

Date: _____ Song: _____ Today's Scripture: _____

1. Tell God what you saw in His character of love.
   _____
   _____
   _____
   _____

2. As the greatest revelation of God's love, what picture of Jesus or Him crucified gave you the assurance of salvation today?
   _____
   _____
   _____
   _____

3. In light of your assurance in Christ, what did the Holy Spirit say to you or ask you to do?
   _____
   _____
   _____
   _____

4. Based on what He said, write at least one verse you will meditate on and memorize today?
   _____
   _____
   _____
   _____

Date: _____ Song: _____ Today's Scripture: _____

1. Tell God what you saw in His character of love.

   _____
   _____
   _____
   _____

2. As the greatest revelation of God's love, what picture of Jesus or Him crucified gave you the assurance of salvation today?

   _____
   _____
   _____
   _____

3. In light of your assurance in Christ, what did the Holy Spirit say to you or ask you to do?

   _____
   _____
   _____
   _____

4. Based on what He said, write at least one verse you will meditate on and memorize today?

   _____
   _____
   _____
   _____

Date: _____ Song: _____ Today's Scripture: _____

1. Tell God what you saw in His character of love.
   _____
   _____
   _____
   _____

2. As the greatest revelation of God's love, what picture of Jesus or Him crucified gave you the assurance of salvation today?
   _____
   _____
   _____
   _____

3. In light of your assurance in Christ, what did the Holy Spirit say to you or ask you to do?
   _____
   _____
   _____
   _____

4. Based on what He said, write at least one verse you will meditate on and memorize today?
   _____
   _____
   _____
   _____

Date: _____ Song: _____ Today's Scripture: _____

1. Tell God what you saw in His character of love.

   _____
   _____
   _____
   _____

2. As the greatest revelation of God's love, what picture of Jesus or Him crucified gave you the assurance of salvation today?

   _____
   _____
   _____
   _____

3. In light of your assurance in Christ, what did the Holy Spirit say to you or ask you to do?

   _____
   _____
   _____
   _____

4. Based on what He said, write at least one verse you will meditate on and memorize today?

   _____
   _____
   _____
   _____

Date: _____ Song: _____ Today's Scripture: _____

1. Tell God what you saw in His character of love.
   _____
   _____
   _____
   _____

2. As the greatest revelation of God's love, what picture of Jesus or Him crucified gave you the assurance of salvation today?
   _____
   _____
   _____
   _____

3. In light of your assurance in Christ, what did the Holy Spirit say to you or ask you to do?
   _____
   _____
   _____
   _____

4. Based on what He said, write at least one verse you will meditate on and memorize today?
   _____
   _____
   _____
   _____

Date: _____ Song: _____ Today's Scripture: _____

1. Tell God what you saw in His character of love.

   _____
   _____
   _____
   _____

2. As the greatest revelation of God's love, what picture of Jesus or Him crucified gave you the assurance of salvation today?

   _____
   _____
   _____
   _____

3. In light of your assurance in Christ, what did the Holy Spirit say to you or ask you to do?

   _____
   _____
   _____
   _____

4. Based on what He said, write at least one verse you will meditate on and memorize today?

   _____
   _____
   _____
   _____

Date: _____ Song: _____ Today's Scripture: _____

1. Tell God what you saw in His character of love.

   _____
   _____
   _____
   _____

2. As the greatest revelation of God's love, what picture of Jesus or Him crucified gave you the assurance of salvation today?

   _____
   _____
   _____
   _____

3. In light of your assurance in Christ, what did the Holy Spirit say to you or ask you to do?

   _____
   _____
   _____
   _____

4. Based on what He said, write at least one verse you will meditate on and memorize today?

   _____
   _____
   _____
   _____

Date: _____ Song: _____ Today's Scripture: _____

1. Tell God what you saw in His character of love.

   _____
   _____
   _____
   _____

2. As the greatest revelation of God's love, what picture of Jesus or Him crucified gave you the assurance of salvation today?

   _____
   _____
   _____
   _____

3. In light of your assurance in Christ, what did the Holy Spirit say to you or ask you to do?

   _____
   _____
   _____
   _____

4. Based on what He said, write at least one verse you will meditate on and memorize today?

   _____
   _____
   _____
   _____

Date: _____ Song: _____ Today's Scripture: _____

1. Tell God what you saw in His character of love.

   _____
   _____
   _____
   _____

2. As the greatest revelation of God's love, what picture of Jesus or Him crucified gave you the assurance of salvation today?

   _____
   _____
   _____
   _____

3. In light of your assurance in Christ, what did the Holy Spirit say to you or ask you to do?

   _____
   _____
   _____
   _____

4. Based on what He said, write at least one verse you will meditate on and memorize today?

   _____
   _____
   _____
   _____

Date: _____ Song: _____ Today's Scripture: _____

1. Tell God what you saw in His character of love.

   _____
   _____
   _____
   _____

2. As the greatest revelation of God's love, what picture of Jesus or Him crucified gave you the assurance of salvation today?

   _____
   _____
   _____
   _____

3. In light of your assurance in Christ, what did the Holy Spirit say to you or ask you to do?

   _____
   _____
   _____
   _____

4. Based on what He said, write at least one verse you will meditate on and memorize today?

   _____
   _____
   _____
   _____

Date: _____ Song: _____ Today's Scripture: _____

1. Tell God what you saw in His character of love.

   _____
   _____
   _____
   _____

2. As the greatest revelation of God's love, what picture of Jesus or Him crucified gave you the assurance of salvation today?

   _____
   _____
   _____
   _____

3. In light of your assurance in Christ, what did the Holy Spirit say to you or ask you to do?

   _____
   _____
   _____
   _____

4. Based on what He said, write at least one verse you will meditate on and memorize today?

   _____
   _____
   _____
   _____

Date: _____ Song: _____ Today's Scripture: _____

1. Tell God what you saw in His character of love.

   _____
   _____
   _____
   _____

2. As the greatest revelation of God's love, what picture of Jesus or Him crucified gave you the assurance of salvation today?

   _____
   _____
   _____
   _____

3. In light of your assurance in Christ, what did the Holy Spirit say to you or ask you to do?

   _____
   _____
   _____
   _____

4. Based on what He said, write at least one verse you will meditate on and memorize today?

   _____
   _____
   _____
   _____

Date: _____ Song: _____ Today's Scripture: _____

1. Tell God what you saw in His character of love.
   _____
   _____
   _____
   _____

2. As the greatest revelation of God's love, what picture of Jesus or Him crucified gave you the assurance of salvation today?
   _____
   _____
   _____
   _____

3. In light of your assurance in Christ, what did the Holy Spirit say to you or ask you to do?
   _____
   _____
   _____
   _____

4. Based on what He said, write at least one verse you will meditate on and memorize today?
   _____
   _____
   _____
   _____

Date: _____ Song: _____ Today's Scripture: _____

1. Tell God what you saw in His character of love.

   _____
   _____
   _____
   _____

2. As the greatest revelation of God's love, what picture of Jesus or Him crucified gave you the assurance of salvation today?

   _____
   _____
   _____
   _____

3. In light of your assurance in Christ, what did the Holy Spirit say to you or ask you to do?

   _____
   _____
   _____
   _____

4. Based on what He said, write at least one verse you will meditate on and memorize today?

   _____
   _____
   _____
   _____

Date: _____ Song: _____ Today's Scripture: _____

1. Tell God what you saw in His character of love.

   _____
   _____
   _____
   _____

2. As the greatest revelation of God's love, what picture of Jesus or Him crucified gave you the assurance of salvation today?

   _____
   _____
   _____
   _____

3. In light of your assurance in Christ, what did the Holy Spirit say to you or ask you to do?

   _____
   _____
   _____
   _____

4. Based on what He said, write at least one verse you will meditate on and memorize today?

   _____
   _____
   _____
   _____

Date: _____ Song: _____ Today's Scripture: _____

1. Tell God what you saw in His character of love.

   _____
   _____
   _____
   _____

2. As the greatest revelation of God's love, what picture of Jesus or Him crucified gave you the assurance of salvation today?

   _____
   _____
   _____
   _____

3. In light of your assurance in Christ, what did the Holy Spirit say to you or ask you to do?

   _____
   _____
   _____
   _____

4. Based on what He said, write at least one verse you will meditate on and memorize today?

   _____
   _____
   _____
   _____

Date: _____ Song: _____ Today's Scripture: _____

1. Tell God what you saw in His character of love.
   _____
   _____
   _____
   _____

2. As the greatest revelation of God's love, what picture of Jesus or Him crucified gave you the assurance of salvation today?
   _____
   _____
   _____
   _____

3. In light of your assurance in Christ, what did the Holy Spirit say to you or ask you to do?
   _____
   _____
   _____
   _____

4. Based on what He said, write at least one verse you will meditate on and memorize today?
   _____
   _____
   _____
   _____

Date: _____ Song: _____ Today's Scripture: _____

1. Tell God what you saw in His character of love.

   _____
   _____
   _____
   _____

2. As the greatest revelation of God's love, what picture of Jesus or Him crucified gave you the assurance of salvation today?

   _____
   _____
   _____
   _____

3. In light of your assurance in Christ, what did the Holy Spirit say to you or ask you to do?

   _____
   _____
   _____
   _____

4. Based on what He said, write at least one verse you will meditate on and memorize today?

   _____
   _____
   _____
   _____

Date: _____ Song: _____ Today's Scripture: _____

1. Tell God what you saw in His character of love.
   _____
   _____
   _____
   _____

2. As the greatest revelation of God's love, what picture of Jesus or Him crucified gave you the assurance of salvation today?
   _____
   _____
   _____
   _____

3. In light of your assurance in Christ, what did the Holy Spirit say to you or ask you to do?
   _____
   _____
   _____
   _____

4. Based on what He said, write at least one verse you will meditate on and memorize today?
   _____
   _____
   _____
   _____

Date: _____ Song: _____ Today's Scripture: _____

1. Tell God what you saw in His character of love.

   _____
   _____
   _____
   _____

2. As the greatest revelation of God's love, what picture of Jesus or Him crucified gave you the assurance of salvation today?

   _____
   _____
   _____
   _____

3. In light of your assurance in Christ, what did the Holy Spirit say to you or ask you to do?

   _____
   _____
   _____
   _____

4. Based on what He said, write at least one verse you will meditate on and memorize today?

   _____
   _____
   _____
   _____

Date: _____ Song: _____ Today's Scripture: _____

1. Tell God what you saw in His character of love.
   _____
   _____
   _____
   _____

2. As the greatest revelation of God's love, what picture of Jesus or Him crucified gave you the assurance of salvation today?
   _____
   _____
   _____
   _____

3. In light of your assurance in Christ, what did the Holy Spirit say to you or ask you to do?
   _____
   _____
   _____
   _____

4. Based on what He said, write at least one verse you will meditate on and memorize today?
   _____
   _____
   _____
   _____

Date: _____ Song: _____ Today's Scripture: _____

1. Tell God what you saw in His character of love.

   _____
   _____
   _____
   _____

2. As the greatest revelation of God's love, what picture of Jesus or Him crucified gave you the assurance of salvation today?

   _____
   _____
   _____
   _____

3. In light of your assurance in Christ, what did the Holy Spirit say to you or ask you to do?

   _____
   _____
   _____
   _____

4. Based on what He said, write at least one verse you will meditate on and memorize today?

   _____
   _____
   _____
   _____

Date: _____ Song: _____ Today's Scripture: _____

1. Tell God what you saw in His character of love.

   _____
   _____
   _____
   _____

2. As the greatest revelation of God's love, what picture of Jesus or Him crucified gave you the assurance of salvation today?

   _____
   _____
   _____
   _____

3. In light of your assurance in Christ, what did the Holy Spirit say to you or ask you to do?

   _____
   _____
   _____
   _____

4. Based on what He said, write at least one verse you will meditate on and memorize today?

   _____
   _____
   _____
   _____

Date: _____ Song: _____ Today's Scripture: _____

1. Tell God what you saw in His character of love.

   _____
   _____
   _____
   _____

2. As the greatest revelation of God's love, what picture of Jesus or Him crucified gave you the assurance of salvation today?

   _____
   _____
   _____
   _____

3. In light of your assurance in Christ, what did the Holy Spirit say to you or ask you to do?

   _____
   _____
   _____
   _____

4. Based on what He said, write at least one verse you will meditate on and memorize today?

   _____
   _____
   _____
   _____

Date: _____ Song: _____ Today's Scripture: _____

1. Tell God what you saw in His character of love.
   _____
   _____
   _____
   _____

2. As the greatest revelation of God's love, what picture of Jesus or Him crucified gave you the assurance of salvation today?
   _____
   _____
   _____
   _____

3. In light of your assurance in Christ, what did the Holy Spirit say to you or ask you to do?
   _____
   _____
   _____
   _____

4. Based on what He said, write at least one verse you will meditate on and memorize today?
   _____
   _____
   _____
   _____

Date: _____ Song: _____ Today's Scripture: _____

1. Tell God what you saw in His character of love.

   _____
   _____
   _____
   _____

2. As the greatest revelation of God's love, what picture of Jesus or Him crucified gave you the assurance of salvation today?

   _____
   _____
   _____
   _____

3. In light of your assurance in Christ, what did the Holy Spirit say to you or ask you to do?

   _____
   _____
   _____
   _____

4. Based on what He said, write at least one verse you will meditate on and memorize today?

   _____
   _____
   _____
   _____

Date: _____ Song: _____ Today's Scripture: _____

1. Tell God what you saw in His character of love.
   _____
   _____
   _____
   _____

2. As the greatest revelation of God's love, what picture of Jesus or Him crucified gave you the assurance of salvation today?
   _____
   _____
   _____
   _____

3. In light of your assurance in Christ, what did the Holy Spirit say to you or ask you to do?
   _____
   _____
   _____
   _____

4. Based on what He said, write at least one verse you will meditate on and memorize today?
   _____
   _____
   _____
   _____

Date: _____ Song: _____ Today's Scripture: _____

1. Tell God what you saw in His character of love.

   _____
   _____
   _____
   _____

2. As the greatest revelation of God's love, what picture of Jesus or Him crucified gave you the assurance of salvation today?

   _____
   _____
   _____
   _____

3. In light of your assurance in Christ, what did the Holy Spirit say to you or ask you to do?

   _____
   _____
   _____
   _____

4. Based on what He said, write at least one verse you will meditate on and memorize today?

   _____
   _____
   _____
   _____

Date: _____ Song: _____ Today's Scripture: _____

1. Tell God what you saw in His character of love.
   _____
   _____
   _____
   _____

2. As the greatest revelation of God's love, what picture of Jesus or Him crucified gave you the assurance of salvation today?
   _____
   _____
   _____
   _____

3. In light of your assurance in Christ, what did the Holy Spirit say to you or ask you to do?
   _____
   _____
   _____
   _____

4. Based on what He said, write at least one verse you will meditate on and memorize today?
   _____
   _____
   _____
   _____

Date: _____ Song: _____ Today's Scripture: _____

1. Tell God what you saw in His character of love.

   _____
   _____
   _____
   _____

2. As the greatest revelation of God's love, what picture of Jesus or Him crucified gave you the assurance of salvation today?

   _____
   _____
   _____
   _____

3. In light of your assurance in Christ, what did the Holy Spirit say to you or ask you to do?

   _____
   _____
   _____
   _____

4. Based on what He said, write at least one verse you will meditate on and memorize today?

   _____
   _____
   _____
   _____

Date: _____ Song: _____ Today's Scripture: _____

1. Tell God what you saw in His character of love.

   _____
   _____
   _____
   _____

2. As the greatest revelation of God's love, what picture of Jesus or Him crucified gave you the assurance of salvation today?

   _____
   _____
   _____
   _____

3. In light of your assurance in Christ, what did the Holy Spirit say to you or ask you to do?

   _____
   _____
   _____
   _____

4. Based on what He said, write at least one verse you will meditate on and memorize today?

   _____
   _____
   _____
   _____

Date: _____ Song: _____ Today's Scripture: _____

1. Tell God what you saw in His character of love.

   _____
   _____
   _____
   _____

2. As the greatest revelation of God's love, what picture of Jesus or Him crucified gave you the assurance of salvation today?

   _____
   _____
   _____
   _____

3. In light of your assurance in Christ, what did the Holy Spirit say to you or ask you to do?

   _____
   _____
   _____
   _____

4. Based on what He said, write at least one verse you will meditate on and memorize today?

   _____
   _____
   _____
   _____

Date: _____ Song: _____ Today's Scripture: _____

1. Tell God what you saw in His character of love.
   _____
   _____
   _____
   _____

2. As the greatest revelation of God's love, what picture of Jesus or Him crucified gave you the assurance of salvation today?
   _____
   _____
   _____
   _____

3. In light of your assurance in Christ, what did the Holy Spirit say to you or ask you to do?
   _____
   _____
   _____
   _____

4. Based on what He said, write at least one verse you will meditate on and memorize today?
   _____
   _____
   _____
   _____

Date: _____ Song: _____ Today's Scripture: _____

1. Tell God what you saw in His character of love.

   _____
   _____
   _____
   _____

2. As the greatest revelation of God's love, what picture of Jesus or Him crucified gave you the assurance of salvation today?

   _____
   _____
   _____
   _____

3. In light of your assurance in Christ, what did the Holy Spirit say to you or ask you to do?

   _____
   _____
   _____
   _____

4. Based on what He said, write at least one verse you will meditate on and memorize today?

   _____
   _____
   _____
   _____

Date: _____ Song: _____ Today's Scripture: _____

1. Tell God what you saw in His character of love.
   _____
   _____
   _____
   _____

2. As the greatest revelation of God's love, what picture of Jesus or Him crucified gave you the assurance of salvation today?
   _____
   _____
   _____
   _____

3. In light of your assurance in Christ, what did the Holy Spirit say to you or ask you to do?
   _____
   _____
   _____
   _____

4. Based on what He said, write at least one verse you will meditate on and memorize today?
   _____
   _____
   _____
   _____

Date: _____ Song: _____ Today's Scripture: _____

1. Tell God what you saw in His character of love.

   _____
   _____
   _____
   _____

2. As the greatest revelation of God's love, what picture of Jesus or Him crucified gave you the assurance of salvation today?

   _____
   _____
   _____
   _____

3. In light of your assurance in Christ, what did the Holy Spirit say to you or ask you to do?

   _____
   _____
   _____
   _____

4. Based on what He said, write at least one verse you will meditate on and memorize today?

   _____
   _____
   _____
   _____

Date: _____ Song: _____ Today's Scripture: _____

1. Tell God what you saw in His character of love.

   _____
   _____
   _____
   _____

2. As the greatest revelation of God's love, what picture of Jesus or Him crucified gave you the assurance of salvation today?

   _____
   _____
   _____
   _____

3. In light of your assurance in Christ, what did the Holy Spirit say to you or ask you to do?

   _____
   _____
   _____
   _____

4. Based on what He said, write at least one verse you will meditate on and memorize today?

   _____
   _____
   _____
   _____

Date: _____ Song: _____ Today's Scripture: _____

1. Tell God what you saw in His character of love.

   _____
   _____
   _____
   _____

2. As the greatest revelation of God's love, what picture of Jesus or Him crucified gave you the assurance of salvation today?

   _____
   _____
   _____
   _____

3. In light of your assurance in Christ, what did the Holy Spirit say to you or ask you to do?

   _____
   _____
   _____
   _____

4. Based on what He said, write at least one verse you will meditate on and memorize today?

   _____
   _____
   _____
   _____

Date: _____ Song: _____ Today's Scripture: _____

1. Tell God what you saw in His character of love.
   _____
   _____
   _____
   _____

2. As the greatest revelation of God's love, what picture of Jesus or Him crucified gave you the assurance of salvation today?
   _____
   _____
   _____
   _____

3. In light of your assurance in Christ, what did the Holy Spirit say to you or ask you to do?
   _____
   _____
   _____
   _____

4. Based on what He said, write at least one verse you will meditate on and memorize today?
   _____
   _____
   _____
   _____

Date: _____ Song: _____ Today's Scripture: _____

1. Tell God what you saw in His character of love.

   _____
   _____
   _____
   _____

2. As the greatest revelation of God's love, what picture of Jesus or Him crucified gave you the assurance of salvation today?

   _____
   _____
   _____
   _____

3. In light of your assurance in Christ, what did the Holy Spirit say to you or ask you to do?

   _____
   _____
   _____
   _____

4. Based on what He said, write at least one verse you will meditate on and memorize today?

   _____
   _____
   _____
   _____

Date: _____ Song: _____ Today's Scripture: _____

1. Tell God what you saw in His character of love.
   _____
   _____
   _____
   _____

2. As the greatest revelation of God's love, what picture of Jesus or Him crucified gave you the assurance of salvation today?
   _____
   _____
   _____
   _____

3. In light of your assurance in Christ, what did the Holy Spirit say to you or ask you to do?
   _____
   _____
   _____
   _____

4. Based on what He said, write at least one verse you will meditate on and memorize today?
   _____
   _____
   _____
   _____

Date: _____ Song: _____ Today's Scripture: _____

1. Tell God what you saw in His character of love.

   _____
   _____
   _____
   _____

2. As the greatest revelation of God's love, what picture of Jesus or Him crucified gave you the assurance of salvation today?

   _____
   _____
   _____
   _____

3. In light of your assurance in Christ, what did the Holy Spirit say to you or ask you to do?

   _____
   _____
   _____
   _____

4. Based on what He said, write at least one verse you will meditate on and memorize today?

   _____
   _____
   _____
   _____

Date: _____ Song: _____ Today's Scripture: _____

1. Tell God what you saw in His character of love.

   _____
   _____
   _____
   _____

2. As the greatest revelation of God's love, what picture of Jesus or Him crucified gave you the assurance of salvation today?

   _____
   _____
   _____
   _____

3. In light of your assurance in Christ, what did the Holy Spirit say to you or ask you to do?

   _____
   _____
   _____
   _____

4. Based on what He said, write at least one verse you will meditate on and memorize today?

   _____
   _____
   _____
   _____

Date: _____ Song: _____ Today's Scripture: _____

1. Tell God what you saw in His character of love.

   _____
   _____
   _____
   _____

2. As the greatest revelation of God's love, what picture of Jesus or Him crucified gave you the assurance of salvation today?

   _____
   _____
   _____
   _____

3. In light of your assurance in Christ, what did the Holy Spirit say to you or ask you to do?

   _____
   _____
   _____
   _____

4. Based on what He said, write at least one verse you will meditate on and memorize today?

   _____
   _____
   _____
   _____

Date: _____ Song: _____ Today's Scripture: _____

1. Tell God what you saw in His character of love.
   _____
   _____
   _____
   _____

2. As the greatest revelation of God's love, what picture of Jesus or Him crucified gave you the assurance of salvation today?
   _____
   _____
   _____
   _____

3. In light of your assurance in Christ, what did the Holy Spirit say to you or ask you to do?
   _____
   _____
   _____
   _____

4. Based on what He said, write at least one verse you will meditate on and memorize today?
   _____
   _____
   _____
   _____

Date: _____ Song: _____ Today's Scripture: _____

1. Tell God what you saw in His character of love.

   _____
   _____
   _____
   _____

2. As the greatest revelation of God's love, what picture of Jesus or Him crucified gave you the assurance of salvation today?

   _____
   _____
   _____
   _____

3. In light of your assurance in Christ, what did the Holy Spirit say to you or ask you to do?

   _____
   _____
   _____
   _____

4. Based on what He said, write at least one verse you will meditate on and memorize today?

   _____
   _____
   _____
   _____

Date: _____ Song: _____ Today's Scripture: _____

1. Tell God what you saw in His character of love.
   _____
   _____
   _____
   _____

2. As the greatest revelation of God's love, what picture of Jesus or Him crucified gave you the assurance of salvation today?
   _____
   _____
   _____
   _____

3. In light of your assurance in Christ, what did the Holy Spirit say to you or ask you to do?
   _____
   _____
   _____
   _____

4. Based on what He said, write at least one verse you will meditate on and memorize today?
   _____
   _____
   _____
   _____

Date: _____ Song: _____ Today's Scripture: _____

1. Tell God what you saw in His character of love.

   _____
   _____
   _____
   _____

2. As the greatest revelation of God's love, what picture of Jesus or Him crucified gave you the assurance of salvation today?

   _____
   _____
   _____
   _____

3. In light of your assurance in Christ, what did the Holy Spirit say to you or ask you to do?

   _____
   _____
   _____
   _____

4. Based on what He said, write at least one verse you will meditate on and memorize today?

   _____
   _____
   _____
   _____

Date: _____ Song: _____ Today's Scripture: _____

1. Tell God what you saw in His character of love.

   _____
   _____
   _____
   _____

2. As the greatest revelation of God's love, what picture of Jesus or Him crucified gave you the assurance of salvation today?

   _____
   _____
   _____
   _____

3. In light of your assurance in Christ, what did the Holy Spirit say to you or ask you to do?

   _____
   _____
   _____
   _____

4. Based on what He said, write at least one verse you will meditate on and memorize today?

   _____
   _____
   _____
   _____

Date: _____ Song: _____ Today's Scripture: _____

1. Tell God what you saw in His character of love.

   _____
   _____
   _____
   _____

2. As the greatest revelation of God's love, what picture of Jesus or Him crucified gave you the assurance of salvation today?

   _____
   _____
   _____
   _____

3. In light of your assurance in Christ, what did the Holy Spirit say to you or ask you to do?

   _____
   _____
   _____
   _____

4. Based on what He said, write at least one verse you will meditate on and memorize today?

   _____
   _____
   _____
   _____

Date: _____ Song: _____ Today's Scripture: _____

1. Tell God what you saw in His character of love.
   _____
   _____
   _____
   _____

2. As the greatest revelation of God's love, what picture of Jesus or Him crucified gave you the assurance of salvation today?
   _____
   _____
   _____
   _____

3. In light of your assurance in Christ, what did the Holy Spirit say to you or ask you to do?
   _____
   _____
   _____
   _____

4. Based on what He said, write at least one verse you will meditate on and memorize today?
   _____
   _____
   _____
   _____

Date: _____ Song: _____ Today's Scripture: _____

1. Tell God what you saw in His character of love.

   _____
   _____
   _____
   _____

2. As the greatest revelation of God's love, what picture of Jesus or Him crucified gave you the assurance of salvation today?

   _____
   _____
   _____
   _____

3. In light of your assurance in Christ, what did the Holy Spirit say to you or ask you to do?

   _____
   _____
   _____
   _____

4. Based on what He said, write at least one verse you will meditate on and memorize today?

   _____
   _____
   _____
   _____

Date: _____ Song: _____ Today's Scripture: _____

1. Tell God what you saw in His character of love.

   _____
   _____
   _____
   _____

2. As the greatest revelation of God's love, what picture of Jesus or Him crucified gave you the assurance of salvation today?

   _____
   _____
   _____
   _____

3. In light of your assurance in Christ, what did the Holy Spirit say to you or ask you to do?

   _____
   _____
   _____
   _____

4. Based on what He said, write at least one verse you will meditate on and memorize today?

   _____
   _____
   _____
   _____

Date: _____ Song: _____ Today's Scripture: _____

1. Tell God what you saw in His character of love.

   _____
   _____
   _____
   _____

2. As the greatest revelation of God's love, what picture of Jesus or Him crucified gave you the assurance of salvation today?

   _____
   _____
   _____
   _____

3. In light of your assurance in Christ, what did the Holy Spirit say to you or ask you to do?

   _____
   _____
   _____
   _____

4. Based on what He said, write at least one verse you will meditate on and memorize today?

   _____
   _____
   _____
   _____

Date: _____ Song: _____ Today's Scripture: _____

1. Tell God what you saw in His character of love.

   _____
   _____
   _____
   _____

2. As the greatest revelation of God's love, what picture of Jesus or Him crucified gave you the assurance of salvation today?

   _____
   _____
   _____
   _____

3. In light of your assurance in Christ, what did the Holy Spirit say to you or ask you to do?

   _____
   _____
   _____
   _____

4. Based on what He said, write at least one verse you will meditate on and memorize today?

   _____
   _____
   _____
   _____

Date: _____ Song: _____ Today's Scripture: _____

1. Tell God what you saw in His character of love.

   _____
   _____
   _____
   _____

2. As the greatest revelation of God's love, what picture of Jesus or Him crucified gave you the assurance of salvation today?

   _____
   _____
   _____
   _____

3. In light of your assurance in Christ, what did the Holy Spirit say to you or ask you to do?

   _____
   _____
   _____
   _____

4. Based on what He said, write at least one verse you will meditate on and memorize today?

   _____
   _____
   _____
   _____

Date: _____ Song: _____ Today's Scripture: _____

1. Tell God what you saw in His character of love.
   _____
   _____
   _____
   _____

2. As the greatest revelation of God's love, what picture of Jesus or Him crucified gave you the assurance of salvation today?
   _____
   _____
   _____
   _____

3. In light of your assurance in Christ, what did the Holy Spirit say to you or ask you to do?
   _____
   _____
   _____
   _____

4. Based on what He said, write at least one verse you will meditate on and memorize today?
   _____
   _____
   _____
   _____

Date: _____ Song: _____ Today's Scripture: _____

1. Tell God what you saw in His character of love.

   _____
   _____
   _____
   _____

2. As the greatest revelation of God's love, what picture of Jesus or Him crucified gave you the assurance of salvation today?

   _____
   _____
   _____
   _____

3. In light of your assurance in Christ, what did the Holy Spirit say to you or ask you to do?

   _____
   _____
   _____
   _____

4. Based on what He said, write at least one verse you will meditate on and memorize today?

   _____
   _____
   _____
   _____

Date: _____ Song: _____ Today's Scripture: _____

1. Tell God what you saw in His character of love.

   _____
   _____
   _____
   _____

2. As the greatest revelation of God's love, what picture of Jesus or Him crucified gave you the assurance of salvation today?

   _____
   _____
   _____
   _____

3. In light of your assurance in Christ, what did the Holy Spirit say to you or ask you to do?

   _____
   _____
   _____
   _____

4. Based on what He said, write at least one verse you will meditate on and memorize today?

   _____
   _____
   _____
   _____

Date: _____ Song: _____ Today's Scripture: _____

1. Tell God what you saw in His character of love.

   _____
   _____
   _____
   _____

2. As the greatest revelation of God's love, what picture of Jesus or Him crucified gave you the assurance of salvation today?

   _____
   _____
   _____
   _____

3. In light of your assurance in Christ, what did the Holy Spirit say to you or ask you to do?

   _____
   _____
   _____
   _____

4. Based on what He said, write at least one verse you will meditate on and memorize today?

   _____
   _____
   _____
   _____

Date: _____ Song: _____ Today's Scripture: _____

1. Tell God what you saw in His character of love.
   _____
   _____
   _____
   _____

2. As the greatest revelation of God's love, what picture of Jesus or Him crucified gave you the assurance of salvation today?
   _____
   _____
   _____
   _____

3. In light of your assurance in Christ, what did the Holy Spirit say to you or ask you to do?
   _____
   _____
   _____
   _____

4. Based on what He said, write at least one verse you will meditate on and memorize today?
   _____
   _____
   _____
   _____

Date: _____ Song: _____ Today's Scripture: _____

1. Tell God what you saw in His character of love.

   _____
   _____
   _____
   _____

2. As the greatest revelation of God's love, what picture of Jesus or Him crucified gave you the assurance of salvation today?

   _____
   _____
   _____
   _____

3. In light of your assurance in Christ, what did the Holy Spirit say to you or ask you to do?

   _____
   _____
   _____
   _____

4. Based on what He said, write at least one verse you will meditate on and memorize today?

   _____
   _____
   _____
   _____

Date: _____ Song: _____ Today's Scripture: _____

1. Tell God what you saw in His character of love.

   _____
   _____
   _____
   _____

2. As the greatest revelation of God's love, what picture of Jesus or Him crucified gave you the assurance of salvation today?

   _____
   _____
   _____
   _____

3. In light of your assurance in Christ, what did the Holy Spirit say to you or ask you to do?

   _____
   _____
   _____
   _____

4. Based on what He said, write at least one verse you will meditate on and memorize today?

   _____
   _____
   _____
   _____

Date: _____ Song: _____ Today's Scripture: _____

1. Tell God what you saw in His character of love.

   _____
   _____
   _____
   _____

2. As the greatest revelation of God's love, what picture of Jesus or Him crucified gave you the assurance of salvation today?

   _____
   _____
   _____
   _____

3. In light of your assurance in Christ, what did the Holy Spirit say to you or ask you to do?

   _____
   _____
   _____
   _____

4. Based on what He said, write at least one verse you will meditate on and memorize today?

   _____
   _____
   _____
   _____

Date: _____ Song: _____ Today's Scripture: _____

1. Tell God what you saw in His character of love.
   _____
   _____
   _____
   _____

2. As the greatest revelation of God's love, what picture of Jesus or Him crucified gave you the assurance of salvation today?
   _____
   _____
   _____
   _____

3. In light of your assurance in Christ, what did the Holy Spirit say to you or ask you to do?
   _____
   _____
   _____
   _____

4. Based on what He said, write at least one verse you will meditate on and memorize today?
   _____
   _____
   _____
   _____

Date: _____ Song: _____ Today's Scripture: _____

1. Tell God what you saw in His character of love.

   _____
   _____
   _____
   _____

2. As the greatest revelation of God's love, what picture of Jesus or Him crucified gave you the assurance of salvation today?

   _____
   _____
   _____
   _____

3. In light of your assurance in Christ, what did the Holy Spirit say to you or ask you to do?

   _____
   _____
   _____
   _____

4. Based on what He said, write at least one verse you will meditate on and memorize today?

   _____
   _____
   _____
   _____

Date: _____ Song: _____ Today's Scripture: _____

1. Tell God what you saw in His character of love.

   _____
   _____
   _____
   _____

2. As the greatest revelation of God's love, what picture of Jesus or Him crucified gave you the assurance of salvation today?

   _____
   _____
   _____
   _____

3. In light of your assurance in Christ, what did the Holy Spirit say to you or ask you to do?

   _____
   _____
   _____
   _____

4. Based on what He said, write at least one verse you will meditate on and memorize today?

   _____
   _____
   _____
   _____

Date: _____ Song: _____ Today's Scripture: _____

1. Tell God what you saw in His character of love.

   _____
   _____
   _____
   _____

2. As the greatest revelation of God's love, what picture of Jesus or Him crucified gave you the assurance of salvation today?

   _____
   _____
   _____
   _____

3. In light of your assurance in Christ, what did the Holy Spirit say to you or ask you to do?

   _____
   _____
   _____
   _____

4. Based on what He said, write at least one verse you will meditate on and memorize today?

   _____
   _____
   _____
   _____

Date: _____ Song: _____ Today's Scripture: _____

1. Tell God what you saw in His character of love.

   _____
   _____
   _____
   _____

2. As the greatest revelation of God's love, what picture of Jesus or Him crucified gave you the assurance of salvation today?

   _____
   _____
   _____
   _____

3. In light of your assurance in Christ, what did the Holy Spirit say to you or ask you to do?

   _____
   _____
   _____
   _____

4. Based on what He said, write at least one verse you will meditate on and memorize today?

   _____
   _____
   _____
   _____

Date: _____ Song: _____ Today's Scripture: _____

1. Tell God what you saw in His character of love.

   _____
   _____
   _____
   _____

2. As the greatest revelation of God's love, what picture of Jesus or Him crucified gave you the assurance of salvation today?

   _____
   _____
   _____
   _____

3. In light of your assurance in Christ, what did the Holy Spirit say to you or ask you to do?

   _____
   _____
   _____
   _____

4. Based on what He said, write at least one verse you will meditate on and memorize today?

   _____
   _____
   _____
   _____

Date: _____ Song: _____ Today's Scripture: _____

1. Tell God what you saw in His character of love.
   _____
   _____
   _____
   _____

2. As the greatest revelation of God's love, what picture of Jesus or Him crucified gave you the assurance of salvation today?
   _____
   _____
   _____
   _____

3. In light of your assurance in Christ, what did the Holy Spirit say to you or ask you to do?
   _____
   _____
   _____
   _____

4. Based on what He said, write at least one verse you will meditate on and memorize today?
   _____
   _____
   _____
   _____

Date: _____ Song: _____ Today's Scripture: _____

1. Tell God what you saw in His character of love.

   _____
   _____
   _____
   _____

2. As the greatest revelation of God's love, what picture of Jesus or Him crucified gave you the assurance of salvation today?

   _____
   _____
   _____
   _____

3. In light of your assurance in Christ, what did the Holy Spirit say to you or ask you to do?

   _____
   _____
   _____
   _____

4. Based on what He said, write at least one verse you will meditate on and memorize today?

   _____
   _____
   _____
   _____

Date: _____ Song: _____ Today's Scripture: _____

1. Tell God what you saw in His character of love.
   _____
   _____
   _____
   _____

2. As the greatest revelation of God's love, what picture of Jesus or Him crucified gave you the assurance of salvation today?
   _____
   _____
   _____
   _____

3. In light of your assurance in Christ, what did the Holy Spirit say to you or ask you to do?
   _____
   _____
   _____
   _____

4. Based on what He said, write at least one verse you will meditate on and memorize today?
   _____
   _____
   _____
   _____

Date: _____ Song: _____ Today's Scripture: _____

1. Tell God what you saw in His character of love.

   _____
   _____
   _____
   _____

2. As the greatest revelation of God's love, what picture of Jesus or Him crucified gave you the assurance of salvation today?

   _____
   _____
   _____
   _____

3. In light of your assurance in Christ, what did the Holy Spirit say to you or ask you to do?

   _____
   _____
   _____
   _____

4. Based on what He said, write at least one verse you will meditate on and memorize today?

   _____
   _____
   _____
   _____

Date: _____ Song: _____ Today's Scripture: _____

1. Tell God what you saw in His character of love.
   _____
   _____
   _____
   _____

2. As the greatest revelation of God's love, what picture of Jesus or Him crucified gave you the assurance of salvation today?
   _____
   _____
   _____
   _____

3. In light of your assurance in Christ, what did the Holy Spirit say to you or ask you to do?
   _____
   _____
   _____
   _____

4. Based on what He said, write at least one verse you will meditate on and memorize today?
   _____
   _____
   _____
   _____

Date: _____ Song: _____ Today's Scripture: _____

1. Tell God what you saw in His character of love.

   _____
   _____
   _____
   _____

2. As the greatest revelation of God's love, what picture of Jesus or Him crucified gave you the assurance of salvation today?

   _____
   _____
   _____
   _____

3. In light of your assurance in Christ, what did the Holy Spirit say to you or ask you to do?

   _____
   _____
   _____
   _____

4. Based on what He said, write at least one verse you will meditate on and memorize today?

   _____
   _____
   _____
   _____

Date: _____ Song: _____ Today's Scripture: _____

1. Tell God what you saw in His character of love.
   _____
   _____
   _____
   _____

2. As the greatest revelation of God's love, what picture of Jesus or Him crucified gave you the assurance of salvation today?
   _____
   _____
   _____
   _____

3. In light of your assurance in Christ, what did the Holy Spirit say to you or ask you to do?
   _____
   _____
   _____
   _____

4. Based on what He said, write at least one verse you will meditate on and memorize today?
   _____
   _____
   _____
   _____

Date: _____ Song: _____ Today's Scripture: _____

1. Tell God what you saw in His character of love.

   _____
   _____
   _____
   _____

2. As the greatest revelation of God's love, what picture of Jesus or Him crucified gave you the assurance of salvation today?

   _____
   _____
   _____
   _____

3. In light of your assurance in Christ, what did the Holy Spirit say to you or ask you to do?

   _____
   _____
   _____
   _____

4. Based on what He said, write at least one verse you will meditate on and memorize today?

   _____
   _____
   _____
   _____

Date: _____ Song: _____ Today's Scripture: _____

1. Tell God what you saw in His character of love.

   _____
   _____
   _____
   _____

2. As the greatest revelation of God's love, what picture of Jesus or Him crucified gave you the assurance of salvation today?

   _____
   _____
   _____
   _____

3. In light of your assurance in Christ, what did the Holy Spirit say to you or ask you to do?

   _____
   _____
   _____
   _____

4. Based on what He said, write at least one verse you will meditate on and memorize today?

   _____
   _____
   _____
   _____

Date: _____ Song: _____ Today's Scripture: _____

1. Tell God what you saw in His character of love.

   _____
   _____
   _____
   _____

2. As the greatest revelation of God's love, what picture of Jesus or Him crucified gave you the assurance of salvation today?

   _____
   _____
   _____
   _____

3. In light of your assurance in Christ, what did the Holy Spirit say to you or ask you to do?

   _____
   _____
   _____
   _____

4. Based on what He said, write at least one verse you will meditate on and memorize today?

   _____
   _____
   _____
   _____

Date: _____ Song: _____ Today's Scripture: _____

1. Tell God what you saw in His character of love.
   _____
   _____
   _____
   _____

2. As the greatest revelation of God's love, what picture of Jesus or Him crucified gave you the assurance of salvation today?
   _____
   _____
   _____
   _____

3. In light of your assurance in Christ, what did the Holy Spirit say to you or ask you to do?
   _____
   _____
   _____
   _____

4. Based on what He said, write at least one verse you will meditate on and memorize today?
   _____
   _____
   _____
   _____

Date: _____ Song: _____ Today's Scripture: _____

1. Tell God what you saw in His character of love.

   _____
   _____
   _____
   _____

2. As the greatest revelation of God's love, what picture of Jesus or Him crucified gave you the assurance of salvation today?

   _____
   _____
   _____
   _____

3. In light of your assurance in Christ, what did the Holy Spirit say to you or ask you to do?

   _____
   _____
   _____
   _____

4. Based on what He said, write at least one verse you will meditate on and memorize today?

   _____
   _____
   _____
   _____

Date: _____ Song: _____ Today's Scripture: _____

1. Tell God what you saw in His character of love.
   _____
   _____
   _____
   _____

2. As the greatest revelation of God's love, what picture of Jesus or Him crucified gave you the assurance of salvation today?
   _____
   _____
   _____
   _____

3. In light of your assurance in Christ, what did the Holy Spirit say to you or ask you to do?
   _____
   _____
   _____
   _____

4. Based on what He said, write at least one verse you will meditate on and memorize today?
   _____
   _____
   _____
   _____

Date: _____ Song: _____ Today's Scripture: _____

1. Tell God what you saw in His character of love.

   _____
   _____
   _____
   _____

2. As the greatest revelation of God's love, what picture of Jesus or Him crucified gave you the assurance of salvation today?

   _____
   _____
   _____
   _____

3. In light of your assurance in Christ, what did the Holy Spirit say to you or ask you to do?

   _____
   _____
   _____
   _____

4. Based on what He said, write at least one verse you will meditate on and memorize today?

   _____
   _____
   _____
   _____

Date: _____ Song: _____ Today's Scripture: _____

1. Tell God what you saw in His character of love.

   _____
   _____
   _____
   _____

2. As the greatest revelation of God's love, what picture of Jesus or Him crucified gave you the assurance of salvation today?

   _____
   _____
   _____
   _____

3. In light of your assurance in Christ, what did the Holy Spirit say to you or ask you to do?

   _____
   _____
   _____
   _____

4. Based on what He said, write at least one verse you will meditate on and memorize today?

   _____
   _____
   _____
   _____

Date: _____ Song: _____ Today's Scripture: _____

1. Tell God what you saw in His character of love.

   _____
   _____
   _____
   _____

2. As the greatest revelation of God's love, what picture of Jesus or Him crucified gave you the assurance of salvation today?

   _____
   _____
   _____
   _____

3. In light of your assurance in Christ, what did the Holy Spirit say to you or ask you to do?

   _____
   _____
   _____
   _____

4. Based on what He said, write at least one verse you will meditate on and memorize today?

   _____
   _____
   _____
   _____

Date: _____ Song: _____ Today's Scripture: _____

1. Tell God what you saw in His character of love.
   _____
   _____
   _____
   _____

2. As the greatest revelation of God's love, what picture of Jesus or Him crucified gave you the assurance of salvation today?
   _____
   _____
   _____
   _____

3. In light of your assurance in Christ, what did the Holy Spirit say to you or ask you to do?
   _____
   _____
   _____
   _____

4. Based on what He said, write at least one verse you will meditate on and memorize today?
   _____
   _____
   _____
   _____

Date: _____ Song: _____ Today's Scripture: _____

1. Tell God what you saw in His character of love.

   _____
   _____
   _____
   _____

2. As the greatest revelation of God's love, what picture of Jesus or Him crucified gave you the assurance of salvation today?

   _____
   _____
   _____
   _____

3. In light of your assurance in Christ, what did the Holy Spirit say to you or ask you to do?

   _____
   _____
   _____
   _____

4. Based on what He said, write at least one verse you will meditate on and memorize today?

   _____
   _____
   _____
   _____

Date: _____ Song: _____ Today's Scripture: _____

1. Tell God what you saw in His character of love.
   _____
   _____
   _____
   _____

2. As the greatest revelation of God's love, what picture of Jesus or Him crucified gave you the assurance of salvation today?
   _____
   _____
   _____
   _____

3. In light of your assurance in Christ, what did the Holy Spirit say to you or ask you to do?
   _____
   _____
   _____
   _____

4. Based on what He said, write at least one verse you will meditate on and memorize today?
   _____
   _____
   _____
   _____

Date: _____ Song: _____ Today's Scripture: _____

1. Tell God what you saw in His character of love.

   _____
   _____
   _____
   _____

2. As the greatest revelation of God's love, what picture of Jesus or Him crucified gave you the assurance of salvation today?

   _____
   _____
   _____
   _____

3. In light of your assurance in Christ, what did the Holy Spirit say to you or ask you to do?

   _____
   _____
   _____
   _____

4. Based on what He said, write at least one verse you will meditate on and memorize today?

   _____
   _____
   _____
   _____

Date: _____ Song: _____ Today's Scripture: _____

1. Tell God what you saw in His character of love.
   _____
   _____
   _____
   _____

2. As the greatest revelation of God's love, what picture of Jesus or Him crucified gave you the assurance of salvation today?
   _____
   _____
   _____
   _____

3. In light of your assurance in Christ, what did the Holy Spirit say to you or ask you to do?
   _____
   _____
   _____
   _____

4. Based on what He said, write at least one verse you will meditate on and memorize today?
   _____
   _____
   _____
   _____

Date: _____ Song: _____ Today's Scripture: _____

1. Tell God what you saw in His character of love.

   _____
   _____
   _____
   _____

2. As the greatest revelation of God's love, what picture of Jesus or Him crucified gave you the assurance of salvation today?

   _____
   _____
   _____
   _____

3. In light of your assurance in Christ, what did the Holy Spirit say to you or ask you to do?

   _____
   _____
   _____
   _____

4. Based on what He said, write at least one verse you will meditate on and memorize today?

   _____
   _____
   _____
   _____

Date: _____ Song: _____ Today's Scripture: _____

1. Tell God what you saw in His character of love.
   _____
   _____
   _____
   _____

2. As the greatest revelation of God's love, what picture of Jesus or Him crucified gave you the assurance of salvation today?
   _____
   _____
   _____
   _____

3. In light of your assurance in Christ, what did the Holy Spirit say to you or ask you to do?
   _____
   _____
   _____
   _____

4. Based on what He said, write at least one verse you will meditate on and memorize today?
   _____
   _____
   _____
   _____

Date: _____ Song: _____ Today's Scripture: _____

1. Tell God what you saw in His character of love.

   _____
   _____
   _____
   _____

2. As the greatest revelation of God's love, what picture of Jesus or Him crucified gave you the assurance of salvation today?

   _____
   _____
   _____
   _____

3. In light of your assurance in Christ, what did the Holy Spirit say to you or ask you to do?

   _____
   _____
   _____
   _____

4. Based on what He said, write at least one verse you will meditate on and memorize today?

   _____
   _____
   _____
   _____

Date: _____ Song: _____ Today's Scripture: _____

1. Tell God what you saw in His character of love.

   _____
   _____
   _____
   _____

2. As the greatest revelation of God's love, what picture of Jesus or Him crucified gave you the assurance of salvation today?

   _____
   _____
   _____
   _____

3. In light of your assurance in Christ, what did the Holy Spirit say to you or ask you to do?

   _____
   _____
   _____
   _____

4. Based on what He said, write at least one verse you will meditate on and memorize today?

   _____
   _____
   _____
   _____

Date: _____ Song: _____ Today's Scripture: _____

1. Tell God what you saw in His character of love.

   _____
   _____
   _____
   _____

2. As the greatest revelation of God's love, what picture of Jesus or Him crucified gave you the assurance of salvation today?

   _____
   _____
   _____
   _____

3. In light of your assurance in Christ, what did the Holy Spirit say to you or ask you to do?

   _____
   _____
   _____
   _____

4. Based on what He said, write at least one verse you will meditate on and memorize today?

   _____
   _____
   _____
   _____

Date: _____ Song: _____ Today's Scripture: _____

1. Tell God what you saw in His character of love.
   _____
   _____
   _____
   _____

2. As the greatest revelation of God's love, what picture of Jesus or Him crucified gave you the assurance of salvation today?
   _____
   _____
   _____
   _____

3. In light of your assurance in Christ, what did the Holy Spirit say to you or ask you to do?
   _____
   _____
   _____
   _____

4. Based on what He said, write at least one verse you will meditate on and memorize today?
   _____
   _____
   _____
   _____

Date: _____ Song: _____ Today's Scripture: _____

1. Tell God what you saw in His character of love.

   _____
   _____
   _____
   _____

2. As the greatest revelation of God's love, what picture of Jesus or Him crucified gave you the assurance of salvation today?

   _____
   _____
   _____
   _____

3. In light of your assurance in Christ, what did the Holy Spirit say to you or ask you to do?

   _____
   _____
   _____
   _____

4. Based on what He said, write at least one verse you will meditate on and memorize today?

   _____
   _____
   _____
   _____

Date: _____ Song: _____ Today's Scripture: _____

1. Tell God what you saw in His character of love.

   _____
   _____
   _____
   _____

2. As the greatest revelation of God's love, what picture of Jesus or Him crucified gave you the assurance of salvation today?

   _____
   _____
   _____
   _____

3. In light of your assurance in Christ, what did the Holy Spirit say to you or ask you to do?

   _____
   _____
   _____
   _____

4. Based on what He said, write at least one verse you will meditate on and memorize today?

   _____
   _____
   _____
   _____

Date: _____ Song: _____ Today's Scripture: _____

1. Tell God what you saw in His character of love.

   _____
   _____
   _____
   _____

2. As the greatest revelation of God's love, what picture of Jesus or Him crucified gave you the assurance of salvation today?

   _____
   _____
   _____
   _____

3. In light of your assurance in Christ, what did the Holy Spirit say to you or ask you to do?

   _____
   _____
   _____
   _____

4. Based on what He said, write at least one verse you will meditate on and memorize today?

   _____
   _____
   _____
   _____

Date: _____ Song: _____ Today's Scripture: _____

1. Tell God what you saw in His character of love.
   _____
   _____
   _____
   _____

2. As the greatest revelation of God's love, what picture of Jesus or Him crucified gave you the assurance of salvation today?
   _____
   _____
   _____
   _____

3. In light of your assurance in Christ, what did the Holy Spirit say to you or ask you to do?
   _____
   _____
   _____
   _____

4. Based on what He said, write at least one verse you will meditate on and memorize today?
   _____
   _____
   _____
   _____

Date: _____ Song: _____ Today's Scripture: _____

1. Tell God what you saw in His character of love.

   _____
   _____
   _____
   _____

2. As the greatest revelation of God's love, what picture of Jesus or Him crucified gave you the assurance of salvation today?

   _____
   _____
   _____
   _____

3. In light of your assurance in Christ, what did the Holy Spirit say to you or ask you to do?

   _____
   _____
   _____
   _____

4. Based on what He said, write at least one verse you will meditate on and memorize today?

   _____
   _____
   _____
   _____

Date: _____ Song: _____ Today's Scripture: _____

1. Tell God what you saw in His character of love.
   _____
   _____
   _____
   _____

2. As the greatest revelation of God's love, what picture of Jesus or Him crucified gave you the assurance of salvation today?
   _____
   _____
   _____
   _____

3. In light of your assurance in Christ, what did the Holy Spirit say to you or ask you to do?
   _____
   _____
   _____
   _____

4. Based on what He said, write at least one verse you will meditate on and memorize today?
   _____
   _____
   _____
   _____

Date: _____ Song: _____ Today's Scripture: _____

1. Tell God what you saw in His character of love.

   _____
   _____
   _____
   _____

2. As the greatest revelation of God's love, what picture of Jesus or Him crucified gave you the assurance of salvation today?

   _____
   _____
   _____
   _____

3. In light of your assurance in Christ, what did the Holy Spirit say to you or ask you to do?

   _____
   _____
   _____
   _____

4. Based on what He said, write at least one verse you will meditate on and memorize today?

   _____
   _____
   _____
   _____

Date: _____ Song: _____ Today's Scripture: _____

1. Tell God what you saw in His character of love.

   _____
   _____
   _____
   _____

2. As the greatest revelation of God's love, what picture of Jesus or Him crucified gave you the assurance of salvation today?

   _____
   _____
   _____
   _____

3. In light of your assurance in Christ, what did the Holy Spirit say to you or ask you to do?

   _____
   _____
   _____
   _____

4. Based on what He said, write at least one verse you will meditate on and memorize today?

   _____
   _____
   _____
   _____

Date: _____ Song: _____ Today's Scripture: _____

1. Tell God what you saw in His character of love.

   _____
   _____
   _____
   _____

2. As the greatest revelation of God's love, what picture of Jesus or Him crucified gave you the assurance of salvation today?

   _____
   _____
   _____
   _____

3. In light of your assurance in Christ, what did the Holy Spirit say to you or ask you to do?

   _____
   _____
   _____
   _____

4. Based on what He said, write at least one verse you will meditate on and memorize today?

   _____
   _____
   _____
   _____

Date: _____ Song: _____ Today's Scripture: _____

1. Tell God what you saw in His character of love.

   _____
   _____
   _____
   _____

2. As the greatest revelation of God's love, what picture of Jesus or Him crucified gave you the assurance of salvation today?

   _____
   _____
   _____
   _____

3. In light of your assurance in Christ, what did the Holy Spirit say to you or ask you to do?

   _____
   _____
   _____
   _____

4. Based on what He said, write at least one verse you will meditate on and memorize today?

   _____
   _____
   _____
   _____

Date: _____ Song: _____ Today's Scripture: _____

1. Tell God what you saw in His character of love.

   _____
   _____
   _____
   _____

2. As the greatest revelation of God's love, what picture of Jesus or Him crucified gave you the assurance of salvation today?

   _____
   _____
   _____
   _____

3. In light of your assurance in Christ, what did the Holy Spirit say to you or ask you to do?

   _____
   _____
   _____
   _____

4. Based on what He said, write at least one verse you will meditate on and memorize today?

   _____
   _____
   _____
   _____

Date: _____ Song: _____ Today's Scripture: _____

1. Tell God what you saw in His character of love.

   _____
   _____
   _____
   _____

2. As the greatest revelation of God's love, what picture of Jesus or Him crucified gave you the assurance of salvation today?

   _____
   _____
   _____
   _____

3. In light of your assurance in Christ, what did the Holy Spirit say to you or ask you to do?

   _____
   _____
   _____
   _____

4. Based on what He said, write at least one verse you will meditate on and memorize today?

   _____
   _____
   _____
   _____

Date: _____ Song: _____ Today's Scripture: _____

1. Tell God what you saw in His character of love.

   _____
   _____
   _____
   _____

2. As the greatest revelation of God's love, what picture of Jesus or Him crucified gave you the assurance of salvation today?

   _____
   _____
   _____
   _____

3. In light of your assurance in Christ, what did the Holy Spirit say to you or ask you to do?

   _____
   _____
   _____
   _____

4. Based on what He said, write at least one verse you will meditate on and memorize today?

   _____
   _____
   _____
   _____

Date: _____ Song: _____ Today's Scripture: _____

1. Tell God what you saw in His character of love.
   _____
   _____
   _____
   _____

2. As the greatest revelation of God's love, what picture of Jesus or Him crucified gave you the assurance of salvation today?
   _____
   _____
   _____
   _____

3. In light of your assurance in Christ, what did the Holy Spirit say to you or ask you to do?
   _____
   _____
   _____
   _____

4. Based on what He said, write at least one verse you will meditate on and memorize today?
   _____
   _____
   _____
   _____

Date: _____ Song: _____ Today's Scripture: _____

1. Tell God what you saw in His character of love.

   _____
   _____
   _____
   _____

2. As the greatest revelation of God's love, what picture of Jesus or Him crucified gave you the assurance of salvation today?

   _____
   _____
   _____
   _____

3. In light of your assurance in Christ, what did the Holy Spirit say to you or ask you to do?

   _____
   _____
   _____
   _____

4. Based on what He said, write at least one verse you will meditate on and memorize today?

   _____
   _____
   _____
   _____

Date: _____ Song: _____ Today's Scripture: _____

1. Tell God what you saw in His character of love.
   _____
   _____
   _____
   _____

2. As the greatest revelation of God's love, what picture of Jesus or Him crucified gave you the assurance of salvation today?
   _____
   _____
   _____
   _____

3. In light of your assurance in Christ, what did the Holy Spirit say to you or ask you to do?
   _____
   _____
   _____
   _____

4. Based on what He said, write at least one verse you will meditate on and memorize today?
   _____
   _____
   _____
   _____

Date: _____ Song: _____ Today's Scripture: _____

1. Tell God what you saw in His character of love.

   _____
   _____
   _____
   _____

2. As the greatest revelation of God's love, what picture of Jesus or Him crucified gave you the assurance of salvation today?

   _____
   _____
   _____
   _____

3. In light of your assurance in Christ, what did the Holy Spirit say to you or ask you to do?

   _____
   _____
   _____
   _____

4. Based on what He said, write at least one verse you will meditate on and memorize today?

   _____
   _____
   _____
   _____

Date: _____ Song: _____ Today's Scripture: _____

1. Tell God what you saw in His character of love.
   _____
   _____
   _____
   _____

2. As the greatest revelation of God's love, what picture of Jesus or Him crucified gave you the assurance of salvation today?
   _____
   _____
   _____
   _____

3. In light of your assurance in Christ, what did the Holy Spirit say to you or ask you to do?
   _____
   _____
   _____
   _____

4. Based on what He said, write at least one verse you will meditate on and memorize today?
   _____
   _____
   _____
   _____

Date: _____ Song: _____ Today's Scripture: _____

1. Tell God what you saw in His character of love.

   _____
   _____
   _____
   _____

2. As the greatest revelation of God's love, what picture of Jesus or Him crucified gave you the assurance of salvation today?

   _____
   _____
   _____
   _____

3. In light of your assurance in Christ, what did the Holy Spirit say to you or ask you to do?

   _____
   _____
   _____
   _____

4. Based on what He said, write at least one verse you will meditate on and memorize today?

   _____
   _____
   _____
   _____

Date: _____ Song: _____ Today's Scripture: _____

1. Tell God what you saw in His character of love.

   _____
   _____
   _____
   _____

2. As the greatest revelation of God's love, what picture of Jesus or Him crucified gave you the assurance of salvation today?

   _____
   _____
   _____
   _____

3. In light of your assurance in Christ, what did the Holy Spirit say to you or ask you to do?

   _____
   _____
   _____
   _____

4. Based on what He said, write at least one verse you will meditate on and memorize today?

   _____
   _____
   _____
   _____

Date: _____ Song: _____ Today's Scripture: _____

1. Tell God what you saw in His character of love.

   _____
   _____
   _____
   _____

2. As the greatest revelation of God's love, what picture of Jesus or Him crucified gave you the assurance of salvation today?

   _____
   _____
   _____
   _____

3. In light of your assurance in Christ, what did the Holy Spirit say to you or ask you to do?

   _____
   _____
   _____
   _____

4. Based on what He said, write at least one verse you will meditate on and memorize today?

   _____
   _____
   _____
   _____

Date: _____ Song: _____ Today's Scripture: _____

1. Tell God what you saw in His character of love.

   _____
   _____
   _____
   _____

2. As the greatest revelation of God's love, what picture of Jesus or Him crucified gave you the assurance of salvation today?

   _____
   _____
   _____
   _____

3. In light of your assurance in Christ, what did the Holy Spirit say to you or ask you to do?

   _____
   _____
   _____
   _____

4. Based on what He said, write at least one verse you will meditate on and memorize today?

   _____
   _____
   _____
   _____

Date: _____ Song: _____ Today's Scripture: _____

1. Tell God what you saw in His character of love.

   _____
   _____
   _____
   _____

2. As the greatest revelation of God's love, what picture of Jesus or Him crucified gave you the assurance of salvation today?

   _____
   _____
   _____
   _____

3. In light of your assurance in Christ, what did the Holy Spirit say to you or ask you to do?

   _____
   _____
   _____
   _____

4. Based on what He said, write at least one verse you will meditate on and memorize today?

   _____
   _____
   _____
   _____

Date: _____ Song: _____ Today's Scripture: _____

1. Tell God what you saw in His character of love.

   _____
   _____
   _____
   _____

2. As the greatest revelation of God's love, what picture of Jesus or Him crucified gave you the assurance of salvation today?

   _____
   _____
   _____
   _____

3. In light of your assurance in Christ, what did the Holy Spirit say to you or ask you to do?

   _____
   _____
   _____
   _____

4. Based on what He said, write at least one verse you will meditate on and memorize today?

   _____
   _____
   _____
   _____

Date: _____ Song: _____ Today's Scripture: _____

1. Tell God what you saw in His character of love.

   _____
   _____
   _____
   _____

2. As the greatest revelation of God's love, what picture of Jesus or Him crucified gave you the assurance of salvation today?

   _____
   _____
   _____
   _____

3. In light of your assurance in Christ, what did the Holy Spirit say to you or ask you to do?

   _____
   _____
   _____
   _____

4. Based on what He said, write at least one verse you will meditate on and memorize today?

   _____
   _____
   _____
   _____

Date: _____ Song: _____ Today's Scripture: _____

1. Tell God what you saw in His character of love.

   _____
   _____
   _____
   _____

2. As the greatest revelation of God's love, what picture of Jesus or Him crucified gave you the assurance of salvation today?

   _____
   _____
   _____
   _____

3. In light of your assurance in Christ, what did the Holy Spirit say to you or ask you to do?

   _____
   _____
   _____
   _____

4. Based on what He said, write at least one verse you will meditate on and memorize today?

   _____
   _____
   _____
   _____

Date: _____ Song: _____ Today's Scripture: _____

1. Tell God what you saw in His character of love.

   _____
   _____
   _____
   _____

2. As the greatest revelation of God's love, what picture of Jesus or Him crucified gave you the assurance of salvation today?

   _____
   _____
   _____
   _____

3. In light of your assurance in Christ, what did the Holy Spirit say to you or ask you to do?

   _____
   _____
   _____
   _____

4. Based on what He said, write at least one verse you will meditate on and memorize today?

   _____
   _____
   _____
   _____

Date: _____ Song: _____ Today's Scripture: _____

1. Tell God what you saw in His character of love.

   _____
   _____
   _____
   _____

2. As the greatest revelation of God's love, what picture of Jesus or Him crucified gave you the assurance of salvation today?

   _____
   _____
   _____
   _____

3. In light of your assurance in Christ, what did the Holy Spirit say to you or ask you to do?

   _____
   _____
   _____
   _____

4. Based on what He said, write at least one verse you will meditate on and memorize today?

   _____
   _____
   _____
   _____

Date: _____ Song: _____ Today's Scripture: _____

1. Tell God what you saw in His character of love.

   _____
   _____
   _____
   _____

2. As the greatest revelation of God's love, what picture of Jesus or Him crucified gave you the assurance of salvation today?

   _____
   _____
   _____
   _____

3. In light of your assurance in Christ, what did the Holy Spirit say to you or ask you to do?

   _____
   _____
   _____
   _____

4. Based on what He said, write at least one verse you will meditate on and memorize today?

   _____
   _____
   _____
   _____

Date: _____ Song: _____ Today's Scripture: _____

1. Tell God what you saw in His character of love.
   _____
   _____
   _____
   _____

2. As the greatest revelation of God's love, what picture of Jesus or Him crucified gave you the assurance of salvation today?
   _____
   _____
   _____
   _____

3. In light of your assurance in Christ, what did the Holy Spirit say to you or ask you to do?
   _____
   _____
   _____
   _____

4. Based on what He said, write at least one verse you will meditate on and memorize today?
   _____
   _____
   _____
   _____

Date: _____ Song: _____ Today's Scripture: _____

1. Tell God what you saw in His character of love.

   _____
   _____
   _____
   _____

2. As the greatest revelation of God's love, what picture of Jesus or Him crucified gave you the assurance of salvation today?

   _____
   _____
   _____
   _____

3. In light of your assurance in Christ, what did the Holy Spirit say to you or ask you to do?

   _____
   _____
   _____
   _____

4. Based on what He said, write at least one verse you will meditate on and memorize today?

   _____
   _____
   _____
   _____

Date: _____ Song: _____ Today's Scripture: _____

1. Tell God what you saw in His character of love.

   _____
   _____
   _____
   _____

2. As the greatest revelation of God's love, what picture of Jesus or Him crucified gave you the assurance of salvation today?

   _____
   _____
   _____
   _____

3. In light of your assurance in Christ, what did the Holy Spirit say to you or ask you to do?

   _____
   _____
   _____
   _____

4. Based on what He said, write at least one verse you will meditate on and memorize today?

   _____
   _____
   _____
   _____

Date: _____ Song: _____ Today's Scripture: _____

1. Tell God what you saw in His character of love.

   _____
   _____
   _____
   _____

2. As the greatest revelation of God's love, what picture of Jesus or Him crucified gave you the assurance of salvation today?

   _____
   _____
   _____
   _____

3. In light of your assurance in Christ, what did the Holy Spirit say to you or ask you to do?

   _____
   _____
   _____
   _____

4. Based on what He said, write at least one verse you will meditate on and memorize today?

   _____
   _____
   _____
   _____

Date: _____ Song: _____ Today's Scripture: _____

1. Tell God what you saw in His character of love.

   _____
   _____
   _____
   _____

2. As the greatest revelation of God's love, what picture of Jesus or Him crucified gave you the assurance of salvation today?

   _____
   _____
   _____
   _____

3. In light of your assurance in Christ, what did the Holy Spirit say to you or ask you to do?

   _____
   _____
   _____
   _____

4. Based on what He said, write at least one verse you will meditate on and memorize today?

   _____
   _____
   _____
   _____

Date: _____ Song: _____ Today's Scripture: _____

1. Tell God what you saw in His character of love.

   _____
   _____
   _____
   _____

2. As the greatest revelation of God's love, what picture of Jesus or Him crucified gave you the assurance of salvation today?

   _____
   _____
   _____
   _____

3. In light of your assurance in Christ, what did the Holy Spirit say to you or ask you to do?

   _____
   _____
   _____
   _____

4. Based on what He said, write at least one verse you will meditate on and memorize today?

   _____
   _____
   _____
   _____

Date: _____ Song: _____ Today's Scripture: _____

1. Tell God what you saw in His character of love.

   _____
   _____
   _____
   _____

2. As the greatest revelation of God's love, what picture of Jesus or Him crucified gave you the assurance of salvation today?

   _____
   _____
   _____
   _____

3. In light of your assurance in Christ, what did the Holy Spirit say to you or ask you to do?

   _____
   _____
   _____
   _____

4. Based on what He said, write at least one verse you will meditate on and memorize today?

   _____
   _____
   _____
   _____

Date: _____ Song: _____ Today's Scripture: _____

1. Tell God what you saw in His character of love.

   _____
   _____
   _____
   _____

2. As the greatest revelation of God's love, what picture of Jesus or Him crucified gave you the assurance of salvation today?

   _____
   _____
   _____
   _____

3. In light of your assurance in Christ, what did the Holy Spirit say to you or ask you to do?

   _____
   _____
   _____
   _____

4. Based on what He said, write at least one verse you will meditate on and memorize today?

   _____
   _____
   _____
   _____

Date: _____ Song: _____ Today's Scripture: _____

1. Tell God what you saw in His character of love.

   _____
   _____
   _____
   _____

2. As the greatest revelation of God's love, what picture of Jesus or Him crucified gave you the assurance of salvation today?

   _____
   _____
   _____
   _____

3. In light of your assurance in Christ, what did the Holy Spirit say to you or ask you to do?

   _____
   _____
   _____
   _____

4. Based on what He said, write at least one verse you will meditate on and memorize today?

   _____
   _____
   _____
   _____

Date: _____ Song: _____ Today's Scripture: _____

1. Tell God what you saw in His character of love.

   _____
   _____
   _____
   _____

2. As the greatest revelation of God's love, what picture of Jesus or Him crucified gave you the assurance of salvation today?

   _____
   _____
   _____
   _____

3. In light of your assurance in Christ, what did the Holy Spirit say to you or ask you to do?

   _____
   _____
   _____
   _____

4. Based on what He said, write at least one verse you will meditate on and memorize today?

   _____
   _____
   _____
   _____

Date: _____ Song: _____ Today's Scripture: _____

1. Tell God what you saw in His character of love.

   _____
   _____
   _____
   _____

2. As the greatest revelation of God's love, what picture of Jesus or Him crucified gave you the assurance of salvation today?

   _____
   _____
   _____
   _____

3. In light of your assurance in Christ, what did the Holy Spirit say to you or ask you to do?

   _____
   _____
   _____
   _____

4. Based on what He said, write at least one verse you will meditate on and memorize today?

   _____
   _____
   _____
   _____

Date: _____ Song: _____ Today's Scripture: _____

1. Tell God what you saw in His character of love.

   _____
   _____
   _____
   _____

2. As the greatest revelation of God's love, what picture of Jesus or Him crucified gave you the assurance of salvation today?

   _____
   _____
   _____
   _____

3. In light of your assurance in Christ, what did the Holy Spirit say to you or ask you to do?

   _____
   _____
   _____
   _____

4. Based on what He said, write at least one verse you will meditate on and memorize today?

   _____
   _____
   _____
   _____

Date: _____ Song: _____ Today's Scripture: _____

1. Tell God what you saw in His character of love.

   _____
   _____
   _____
   _____

2. As the greatest revelation of God's love, what picture of Jesus or Him crucified gave you the assurance of salvation today?

   _____
   _____
   _____
   _____

3. In light of your assurance in Christ, what did the Holy Spirit say to you or ask you to do?

   _____
   _____
   _____
   _____

4. Based on what He said, write at least one verse you will meditate on and memorize today?

   _____
   _____
   _____
   _____

Date: _____ Song: _____ Today's Scripture: _____

1. Tell God what you saw in His character of love.

   _____
   _____
   _____
   _____

2. As the greatest revelation of God's love, what picture of Jesus or Him crucified gave you the assurance of salvation today?

   _____
   _____
   _____
   _____

3. In light of your assurance in Christ, what did the Holy Spirit say to you or ask you to do?

   _____
   _____
   _____
   _____

4. Based on what He said, write at least one verse you will meditate on and memorize today?

   _____
   _____
   _____
   _____

Date: _____ Song: _____ Today's Scripture: _____

1. Tell God what you saw in His character of love.

   _____
   _____
   _____
   _____

2. As the greatest revelation of God's love, what picture of Jesus or Him crucified gave you the assurance of salvation today?

   _____
   _____
   _____
   _____

3. In light of your assurance in Christ, what did the Holy Spirit say to you or ask you to do?

   _____
   _____
   _____
   _____

4. Based on what He said, write at least one verse you will meditate on and memorize today?

   _____
   _____
   _____
   _____

Date: _____ Song: _____ Today's Scripture: _____

1. Tell God what you saw in His character of love.

   _____
   _____
   _____
   _____

2. As the greatest revelation of God's love, what picture of Jesus or Him crucified gave you the assurance of salvation today?

   _____
   _____
   _____
   _____

3. In light of your assurance in Christ, what did the Holy Spirit say to you or ask you to do?

   _____
   _____
   _____
   _____

4. Based on what He said, write at least one verse you will meditate on and memorize today?

   _____
   _____
   _____
   _____

Date: _____ Song: _____ Today's Scripture: _____

1. Tell God what you saw in His character of love.
   _____
   _____
   _____
   _____

2. As the greatest revelation of God's love, what picture of Jesus or Him crucified gave you the assurance of salvation today?
   _____
   _____
   _____
   _____

3. In light of your assurance in Christ, what did the Holy Spirit say to you or ask you to do?
   _____
   _____
   _____
   _____

4. Based on what He said, write at least one verse you will meditate on and memorize today?
   _____
   _____
   _____
   _____

Date: _____ Song: _____ Today's Scripture: _____

1. Tell God what you saw in His character of love.

   _____
   _____
   _____
   _____

2. As the greatest revelation of God's love, what picture of Jesus or Him crucified gave you the assurance of salvation today?

   _____
   _____
   _____
   _____

3. In light of your assurance in Christ, what did the Holy Spirit say to you or ask you to do?

   _____
   _____
   _____
   _____

4. Based on what He said, write at least one verse you will meditate on and memorize today?

   _____
   _____
   _____
   _____

Date: _____ Song: _____ Today's Scripture: _____

1. Tell God what you saw in His character of love.

   _____
   _____
   _____
   _____

2. As the greatest revelation of God's love, what picture of Jesus or Him crucified gave you the assurance of salvation today?

   _____
   _____
   _____
   _____

3. In light of your assurance in Christ, what did the Holy Spirit say to you or ask you to do?

   _____
   _____
   _____
   _____

4. Based on what He said, write at least one verse you will meditate on and memorize today?

   _____
   _____
   _____
   _____

Date: _____ Song: _____ Today's Scripture: _____

1. Tell God what you saw in His character of love.

   _____
   _____
   _____
   _____

2. As the greatest revelation of God's love, what picture of Jesus or Him crucified gave you the assurance of salvation today?

   _____
   _____
   _____
   _____

3. In light of your assurance in Christ, what did the Holy Spirit say to you or ask you to do?

   _____
   _____
   _____
   _____

4. Based on what He said, write at least one verse you will meditate on and memorize today?

   _____
   _____
   _____
   _____

Date: _____ Song: _____ Today's Scripture: _____

1. Tell God what you saw in His character of love.
   _____
   _____
   _____
   _____

2. As the greatest revelation of God's love, what picture of Jesus or Him crucified gave you the assurance of salvation today?
   _____
   _____
   _____
   _____

3. In light of your assurance in Christ, what did the Holy Spirit say to you or ask you to do?
   _____
   _____
   _____
   _____

4. Based on what He said, write at least one verse you will meditate on and memorize today?
   _____
   _____
   _____
   _____

Date: _____ Song: _____ Today's Scripture: _____

1. Tell God what you saw in His character of love.

   _____
   _____
   _____
   _____

2. As the greatest revelation of God's love, what picture of Jesus or Him crucified gave you the assurance of salvation today?

   _____
   _____
   _____
   _____

3. In light of your assurance in Christ, what did the Holy Spirit say to you or ask you to do?

   _____
   _____
   _____
   _____

4. Based on what He said, write at least one verse you will meditate on and memorize today?

   _____
   _____
   _____
   _____

Date: _____ Song: _____ Today's Scripture: _____

1. Tell God what you saw in His character of love.

   _____
   _____
   _____
   _____

2. As the greatest revelation of God's love, what picture of Jesus or Him crucified gave you the assurance of salvation today?

   _____
   _____
   _____
   _____

3. In light of your assurance in Christ, what did the Holy Spirit say to you or ask you to do?

   _____
   _____
   _____
   _____

4. Based on what He said, write at least one verse you will meditate on and memorize today?

   _____
   _____
   _____
   _____

Date: _____ Song: _____ Today's Scripture: _____

1. Tell God what you saw in His character of love.

   _____
   _____
   _____
   _____

2. As the greatest revelation of God's love, what picture of Jesus or Him crucified gave you the assurance of salvation today?

   _____
   _____
   _____
   _____

3. In light of your assurance in Christ, what did the Holy Spirit say to you or ask you to do?

   _____
   _____
   _____
   _____

4. Based on what He said, write at least one verse you will meditate on and memorize today?

   _____
   _____
   _____
   _____

Date: _____ Song: _____ Today's Scripture: _____

1. Tell God what you saw in His character of love.

   _____
   _____
   _____
   _____

2. As the greatest revelation of God's love, what picture of Jesus or Him crucified gave you the assurance of salvation today?

   _____
   _____
   _____
   _____

3. In light of your assurance in Christ, what did the Holy Spirit say to you or ask you to do?

   _____
   _____
   _____
   _____

4. Based on what He said, write at least one verse you will meditate on and memorize today?

   _____
   _____
   _____
   _____

Date: _____ Song: _____ Today's Scripture: _____

1. Tell God what you saw in His character of love.

   _____
   _____
   _____
   _____

2. As the greatest revelation of God's love, what picture of Jesus or Him crucified gave you the assurance of salvation today?

   _____
   _____
   _____
   _____

3. In light of your assurance in Christ, what did the Holy Spirit say to you or ask you to do?

   _____
   _____
   _____
   _____

4. Based on what He said, write at least one verse you will meditate on and memorize today?

   _____
   _____
   _____
   _____

Date: _____ Song: _____ Today's Scripture: _____

1. Tell God what you saw in His character of love.
   _____
   _____
   _____
   _____

2. As the greatest revelation of God's love, what picture of Jesus or Him crucified gave you the assurance of salvation today?
   _____
   _____
   _____
   _____

3. In light of your assurance in Christ, what did the Holy Spirit say to you or ask you to do?
   _____
   _____
   _____
   _____

4. Based on what He said, write at least one verse you will meditate on and memorize today?
   _____
   _____
   _____
   _____

Date: _____ Song: _____ Today's Scripture: _____

1. Tell God what you saw in His character of love.

   _____
   _____
   _____
   _____

2. As the greatest revelation of God's love, what picture of Jesus or Him crucified gave you the assurance of salvation today?

   _____
   _____
   _____
   _____

3. In light of your assurance in Christ, what did the Holy Spirit say to you or ask you to do?

   _____
   _____
   _____
   _____

4. Based on what He said, write at least one verse you will meditate on and memorize today?

   _____
   _____
   _____
   _____

Date: _____ Song: _____ Today's Scripture: _____

1. Tell God what you saw in His character of love.

   _____
   _____
   _____
   _____

2. As the greatest revelation of God's love, what picture of Jesus or Him crucified gave you the assurance of salvation today?

   _____
   _____
   _____
   _____

3. In light of your assurance in Christ, what did the Holy Spirit say to you or ask you to do?

   _____
   _____
   _____
   _____

4. Based on what He said, write at least one verse you will meditate on and memorize today?

   _____
   _____
   _____
   _____

Date: _____ Song: _____ Today's Scripture: _____

1. Tell God what you saw in His character of love.

   _____
   _____
   _____
   _____

2. As the greatest revelation of God's love, what picture of Jesus or Him crucified gave you the assurance of salvation today?

   _____
   _____
   _____
   _____

3. In light of your assurance in Christ, what did the Holy Spirit say to you or ask you to do?

   _____
   _____
   _____
   _____

4. Based on what He said, write at least one verse you will meditate on and memorize today?

   _____
   _____
   _____
   _____

Date: _____ Song: _____ Today's Scripture: _____

1. Tell God what you saw in His character of love.
   _____
   _____
   _____
   _____

2. As the greatest revelation of God's love, what picture of Jesus or Him crucified gave you the assurance of salvation today?
   _____
   _____
   _____
   _____

3. In light of your assurance in Christ, what did the Holy Spirit say to you or ask you to do?
   _____
   _____
   _____
   _____

4. Based on what He said, write at least one verse you will meditate on and memorize today?
   _____
   _____
   _____
   _____

Date: _____ Song: _____ Today's Scripture: _____

1. Tell God what you saw in His character of love.

   _____
   _____
   _____
   _____

2. As the greatest revelation of God's love, what picture of Jesus or Him crucified gave you the assurance of salvation today?

   _____
   _____
   _____
   _____

3. In light of your assurance in Christ, what did the Holy Spirit say to you or ask you to do?

   _____
   _____
   _____
   _____

4. Based on what He said, write at least one verse you will meditate on and memorize today?

   _____
   _____
   _____
   _____

Date: _____ Song: _____ Today's Scripture: _____

1. Tell God what you saw in His character of love.
   _____
   _____
   _____
   _____

2. As the greatest revelation of God's love, what picture of Jesus or Him crucified gave you the assurance of salvation today?
   _____
   _____
   _____
   _____

3. In light of your assurance in Christ, what did the Holy Spirit say to you or ask you to do?
   _____
   _____
   _____
   _____

4. Based on what He said, write at least one verse you will meditate on and memorize today?
   _____
   _____
   _____
   _____

Date: _____ Song: _____ Today's Scripture: _____

1. Tell God what you saw in His character of love.

   _____
   _____
   _____
   _____

2. As the greatest revelation of God's love, what picture of Jesus or Him crucified gave you the assurance of salvation today?

   _____
   _____
   _____
   _____

3. In light of your assurance in Christ, what did the Holy Spirit say to you or ask you to do?

   _____
   _____
   _____
   _____

4. Based on what He said, write at least one verse you will meditate on and memorize today?

   _____
   _____
   _____
   _____

Date: _____ Song: _____ Today's Scripture: _____

1. Tell God what you saw in His character of love.
   _____
   _____
   _____
   _____

2. As the greatest revelation of God's love, what picture of Jesus or Him crucified gave you the assurance of salvation today?
   _____
   _____
   _____
   _____

3. In light of your assurance in Christ, what did the Holy Spirit say to you or ask you to do?
   _____
   _____
   _____
   _____

4. Based on what He said, write at least one verse you will meditate on and memorize today?
   _____
   _____
   _____
   _____

Date: _____ Song: _____ Today's Scripture: _____

1. Tell God what you saw in His character of love.

   _____
   _____
   _____
   _____

2. As the greatest revelation of God's love, what picture of Jesus or Him crucified gave you the assurance of salvation today?

   _____
   _____
   _____
   _____

3. In light of your assurance in Christ, what did the Holy Spirit say to you or ask you to do?

   _____
   _____
   _____
   _____

4. Based on what He said, write at least one verse you will meditate on and memorize today?

   _____
   _____
   _____
   _____

Date: _____ Song: _____ Today's Scripture: _____

1. Tell God what you saw in His character of love.
   _____
   _____
   _____
   _____

2. As the greatest revelation of God's love, what picture of Jesus or Him crucified gave you the assurance of salvation today?
   _____
   _____
   _____
   _____

3. In light of your assurance in Christ, what did the Holy Spirit say to you or ask you to do?
   _____
   _____
   _____
   _____

4. Based on what He said, write at least one verse you will meditate on and memorize today?
   _____
   _____
   _____
   _____

Date: _____ Song: _____ Today's Scripture: _____

1. Tell God what you saw in His character of love.

   _____
   _____
   _____
   _____

2. As the greatest revelation of God's love, what picture of Jesus or Him crucified gave you the assurance of salvation today?

   _____
   _____
   _____
   _____

3. In light of your assurance in Christ, what did the Holy Spirit say to you or ask you to do?

   _____
   _____
   _____
   _____

4. Based on what He said, write at least one verse you will meditate on and memorize today?

   _____
   _____
   _____
   _____

Date: _____ Song: _____ Today's Scripture: _____

1. Tell God what you saw in His character of love.

   _____
   _____
   _____
   _____

2. As the greatest revelation of God's love, what picture of Jesus or Him crucified gave you the assurance of salvation today?

   _____
   _____
   _____
   _____

3. In light of your assurance in Christ, what did the Holy Spirit say to you or ask you to do?

   _____
   _____
   _____
   _____

4. Based on what He said, write at least one verse you will meditate on and memorize today?

   _____
   _____
   _____
   _____

Date: _____ Song: _____ Today's Scripture: _____

1. Tell God what you saw in His character of love.

   _____
   _____
   _____
   _____

2. As the greatest revelation of God's love, what picture of Jesus or Him crucified gave you the assurance of salvation today?

   _____
   _____
   _____
   _____

3. In light of your assurance in Christ, what did the Holy Spirit say to you or ask you to do?

   _____
   _____
   _____
   _____

4. Based on what He said, write at least one verse you will meditate on and memorize today?

   _____
   _____
   _____
   _____

Date: _____ Song: _____ Today's Scripture: _____

1. Tell God what you saw in His character of love.

   _____
   _____
   _____
   _____

2. As the greatest revelation of God's love, what picture of Jesus or Him crucified gave you the assurance of salvation today?

   _____
   _____
   _____
   _____

3. In light of your assurance in Christ, what did the Holy Spirit say to you or ask you to do?

   _____
   _____
   _____
   _____

4. Based on what He said, write at least one verse you will meditate on and memorize today?

   _____
   _____
   _____
   _____

Date: _____ Song: _____ Today's Scripture: _____

1. Tell God what you saw in His character of love.

   _____
   _____
   _____
   _____

2. As the greatest revelation of God's love, what picture of Jesus or Him crucified gave you the assurance of salvation today?

   _____
   _____
   _____
   _____

3. In light of your assurance in Christ, what did the Holy Spirit say to you or ask you to do?

   _____
   _____
   _____
   _____

4. Based on what He said, write at least one verse you will meditate on and memorize today?

   _____
   _____
   _____
   _____

Date: _____ Song: _____ Today's Scripture: _____

1. Tell God what you saw in His character of love.

   _____
   _____
   _____
   _____

2. As the greatest revelation of God's love, what picture of Jesus or Him crucified gave you the assurance of salvation today?

   _____
   _____
   _____
   _____

3. In light of your assurance in Christ, what did the Holy Spirit say to you or ask you to do?

   _____
   _____
   _____
   _____

4. Based on what He said, write at least one verse you will meditate on and memorize today?

   _____
   _____
   _____
   _____

Date: _____ Song: _____ Today's Scripture: _____

1. Tell God what you saw in His character of love.

   _____
   _____
   _____
   _____

2. As the greatest revelation of God's love, what picture of Jesus or Him crucified gave you the assurance of salvation today?

   _____
   _____
   _____
   _____

3. In light of your assurance in Christ, what did the Holy Spirit say to you or ask you to do?

   _____
   _____
   _____
   _____

4. Based on what He said, write at least one verse you will meditate on and memorize today?

   _____
   _____
   _____
   _____

Date: _____ Song: _____ Today's Scripture: _____

1. Tell God what you saw in His character of love.

   _____
   _____
   _____
   _____

2. As the greatest revelation of God's love, what picture of Jesus or Him crucified gave you the assurance of salvation today?

   _____
   _____
   _____
   _____

3. In light of your assurance in Christ, what did the Holy Spirit say to you or ask you to do?

   _____
   _____
   _____
   _____

4. Based on what He said, write at least one verse you will meditate on and memorize today?

   _____
   _____
   _____
   _____

Date: _____ Song: _____ Today's Scripture: _____

1. Tell God what you saw in His character of love.

   _____
   _____
   _____
   _____

2. As the greatest revelation of God's love, what picture of Jesus or Him crucified gave you the assurance of salvation today?

   _____
   _____
   _____
   _____

3. In light of your assurance in Christ, what did the Holy Spirit say to you or ask you to do?

   _____
   _____
   _____
   _____

4. Based on what He said, write at least one verse you will meditate on and memorize today?

   _____
   _____
   _____
   _____

Date: _____ Song: _____ Today's Scripture: _____

1. Tell God what you saw in His character of love.

   _____
   _____
   _____
   _____

2. As the greatest revelation of God's love, what picture of Jesus or Him crucified gave you the assurance of salvation today?

   _____
   _____
   _____
   _____

3. In light of your assurance in Christ, what did the Holy Spirit say to you or ask you to do?

   _____
   _____
   _____
   _____

4. Based on what He said, write at least one verse you will meditate on and memorize today?

   _____
   _____
   _____
   _____

Date: _____ Song: _____ Today's Scripture: _____

1. Tell God what you saw in His character of love.

   _____
   _____
   _____
   _____

2. As the greatest revelation of God's love, what picture of Jesus or Him crucified gave you the assurance of salvation today?

   _____
   _____
   _____
   _____

3. In light of your assurance in Christ, what did the Holy Spirit say to you or ask you to do?

   _____
   _____
   _____
   _____

4. Based on what He said, write at least one verse you will meditate on and memorize today?

   _____
   _____
   _____
   _____

Date: _____ Song: _____ Today's Scripture: _____

1. Tell God what you saw in His character of love.

   _____
   _____
   _____
   _____

2. As the greatest revelation of God's love, what picture of Jesus or Him crucified gave you the assurance of salvation today?

   _____
   _____
   _____
   _____

3. In light of your assurance in Christ, what did the Holy Spirit say to you or ask you to do?

   _____
   _____
   _____
   _____

4. Based on what He said, write at least one verse you will meditate on and memorize today?

   _____
   _____
   _____
   _____

Date: _____ Song: _____ Today's Scripture: _____

1. Tell God what you saw in His character of love.

   _____
   _____
   _____
   _____

2. As the greatest revelation of God's love, what picture of Jesus or Him crucified gave you the assurance of salvation today?

   _____
   _____
   _____
   _____

3. In light of your assurance in Christ, what did the Holy Spirit say to you or ask you to do?

   _____
   _____
   _____
   _____

4. Based on what He said, write at least one verse you will meditate on and memorize today?

   _____
   _____
   _____
   _____

Date: _____ Song: _____ Today's Scripture: _____

1. Tell God what you saw in His character of love.

   _____
   _____
   _____
   _____

2. As the greatest revelation of God's love, what picture of Jesus or Him crucified gave you the assurance of salvation today?

   _____
   _____
   _____
   _____

3. In light of your assurance in Christ, what did the Holy Spirit say to you or ask you to do?

   _____
   _____
   _____
   _____

4. Based on what He said, write at least one verse you will meditate on and memorize today?

   _____
   _____
   _____
   _____

Date: _____ Song: _____ Today's Scripture: _____

1. Tell God what you saw in His character of love.

   _____
   _____
   _____
   _____

2. As the greatest revelation of God's love, what picture of Jesus or Him crucified gave you the assurance of salvation today?

   _____
   _____
   _____
   _____

3. In light of your assurance in Christ, what did the Holy Spirit say to you or ask you to do?

   _____
   _____
   _____
   _____

4. Based on what He said, write at least one verse you will meditate on and memorize today?

   _____
   _____
   _____
   _____

Date: _____ Song: _____ Today's Scripture: _____

1. Tell God what you saw in His character of love.

   _____
   _____
   _____
   _____

2. As the greatest revelation of God's love, what picture of Jesus or Him crucified gave you the assurance of salvation today?

   _____
   _____
   _____
   _____

3. In light of your assurance in Christ, what did the Holy Spirit say to you or ask you to do?

   _____
   _____
   _____
   _____

4. Based on what He said, write at least one verse you will meditate on and memorize today?

   _____
   _____
   _____
   _____

Date: _____ Song: _____ Today's Scripture: _____

1. Tell God what you saw in His character of love.

   _____
   _____
   _____
   _____

2. As the greatest revelation of God's love, what picture of Jesus or Him crucified gave you the assurance of salvation today?

   _____
   _____
   _____
   _____

3. In light of your assurance in Christ, what did the Holy Spirit say to you or ask you to do?

   _____
   _____
   _____
   _____

4. Based on what He said, write at least one verse you will meditate on and memorize today?

   _____
   _____
   _____
   _____

Date: _____ Song: _____ Today's Scripture: _____

1. Tell God what you saw in His character of love.

   _____
   _____
   _____
   _____

2. As the greatest revelation of God's love, what picture of Jesus or Him crucified gave you the assurance of salvation today?

   _____
   _____
   _____
   _____

3. In light of your assurance in Christ, what did the Holy Spirit say to you or ask you to do?

   _____
   _____
   _____
   _____

4. Based on what He said, write at least one verse you will meditate on and memorize today?

   _____
   _____
   _____
   _____

Date: _____ Song: _____ Today's Scripture: _____

1. Tell God what you saw in His character of love.

   _____
   _____
   _____
   _____

2. As the greatest revelation of God's love, what picture of Jesus or Him crucified gave you the assurance of salvation today?

   _____
   _____
   _____
   _____

3. In light of your assurance in Christ, what did the Holy Spirit say to you or ask you to do?

   _____
   _____
   _____
   _____

4. Based on what He said, write at least one verse you will meditate on and memorize today?

   _____
   _____
   _____
   _____

Date: _____ Song: _____ Today's Scripture: _____

1. Tell God what you saw in His character of love.
   _____
   _____
   _____
   _____

2. As the greatest revelation of God's love, what picture of Jesus or Him crucified gave you the assurance of salvation today?
   _____
   _____
   _____
   _____

3. In light of your assurance in Christ, what did the Holy Spirit say to you or ask you to do?
   _____
   _____
   _____
   _____

4. Based on what He said, write at least one verse you will meditate on and memorize today?
   _____
   _____
   _____
   _____

Date: _____ Song: _____ Today's Scripture: _____

1. Tell God what you saw in His character of love.

   _____
   _____
   _____
   _____

2. As the greatest revelation of God's love, what picture of Jesus or Him crucified gave you the assurance of salvation today?

   _____
   _____
   _____
   _____

3. In light of your assurance in Christ, what did the Holy Spirit say to you or ask you to do?

   _____
   _____
   _____
   _____

4. Based on what He said, write at least one verse you will meditate on and memorize today?

   _____
   _____
   _____
   _____

Date: _____ Song: _____ Today's Scripture: _____

1. Tell God what you saw in His character of love.

   _____
   _____
   _____
   _____

2. As the greatest revelation of God's love, what picture of Jesus or Him crucified gave you the assurance of salvation today?

   _____
   _____
   _____
   _____

3. In light of your assurance in Christ, what did the Holy Spirit say to you or ask you to do?

   _____
   _____
   _____
   _____

4. Based on what He said, write at least one verse you will meditate on and memorize today?

   _____
   _____
   _____
   _____

Date: _____ Song: _____ Today's Scripture: _____

1. Tell God what you saw in His character of love.

   _____
   _____
   _____
   _____

2. As the greatest revelation of God's love, what picture of Jesus or Him crucified gave you the assurance of salvation today?

   _____
   _____
   _____
   _____

3. In light of your assurance in Christ, what did the Holy Spirit say to you or ask you to do?

   _____
   _____
   _____
   _____

4. Based on what He said, write at least one verse you will meditate on and memorize today?

   _____
   _____
   _____
   _____

Date: _____ Song: _____ Today's Scripture: _____

1. Tell God what you saw in His character of love.

   _____
   _____
   _____
   _____

2. As the greatest revelation of God's love, what picture of Jesus or Him crucified gave you the assurance of salvation today?

   _____
   _____
   _____
   _____

3. In light of your assurance in Christ, what did the Holy Spirit say to you or ask you to do?

   _____
   _____
   _____
   _____

4. Based on what He said, write at least one verse you will meditate on and memorize today?

   _____
   _____
   _____
   _____

Date: _____ Song: _____ Today's Scripture: _____

1. Tell God what you saw in His character of love.

   _____
   _____
   _____
   _____

2. As the greatest revelation of God's love, what picture of Jesus or Him crucified gave you the assurance of salvation today?

   _____
   _____
   _____
   _____

3. In light of your assurance in Christ, what did the Holy Spirit say to you or ask you to do?

   _____
   _____
   _____
   _____

4. Based on what He said, write at least one verse you will meditate on and memorize today?

   _____
   _____
   _____
   _____

Date: _____ Song: _____ Today's Scripture: _____

1. Tell God what you saw in His character of love.

   _____
   _____
   _____
   _____

2. As the greatest revelation of God's love, what picture of Jesus or Him crucified gave you the assurance of salvation today?

   _____
   _____
   _____
   _____

3. In light of your assurance in Christ, what did the Holy Spirit say to you or ask you to do?

   _____
   _____
   _____
   _____

4. Based on what He said, write at least one verse you will meditate on and memorize today?

   _____
   _____
   _____
   _____

Date: _____ Song: _____ Today's Scripture: _____

1. Tell God what you saw in His character of love.

   _____
   _____
   _____
   _____

2. As the greatest revelation of God's love, what picture of Jesus or Him crucified gave you the assurance of salvation today?

   _____
   _____
   _____
   _____

3. In light of your assurance in Christ, what did the Holy Spirit say to you or ask you to do?

   _____
   _____
   _____
   _____

4. Based on what He said, write at least one verse you will meditate on and memorize today?

   _____
   _____
   _____
   _____

Date: _____ Song: _____ Today's Scripture: _____

1. Tell God what you saw in His character of love.

   _____
   _____
   _____
   _____

2. As the greatest revelation of God's love, what picture of Jesus or Him crucified gave you the assurance of salvation today?

   _____
   _____
   _____
   _____

3. In light of your assurance in Christ, what did the Holy Spirit say to you or ask you to do?

   _____
   _____
   _____
   _____

4. Based on what He said, write at least one verse you will meditate on and memorize today?

   _____
   _____
   _____
   _____

Date: _____ Song: _____ Today's Scripture: _____

1. Tell God what you saw in His character of love.

   _____
   _____
   _____
   _____

2. As the greatest revelation of God's love, what picture of Jesus or Him crucified gave you the assurance of salvation today?

   _____
   _____
   _____
   _____

3. In light of your assurance in Christ, what did the Holy Spirit say to you or ask you to do?

   _____
   _____
   _____
   _____

4. Based on what He said, write at least one verse you will meditate on and memorize today?

   _____
   _____
   _____
   _____

Date: _____ Song: _____ Today's Scripture: _____

1. Tell God what you saw in His character of love.
   _____
   _____
   _____
   _____

2. As the greatest revelation of God's love, what picture of Jesus or Him crucified gave you the assurance of salvation today?
   _____
   _____
   _____
   _____

3. In light of your assurance in Christ, what did the Holy Spirit say to you or ask you to do?
   _____
   _____
   _____
   _____

4. Based on what He said, write at least one verse you will meditate on and memorize today?
   _____
   _____
   _____
   _____

Date: _____ Song: _____ Today's Scripture: _____

1. Tell God what you saw in His character of love.

   _____
   _____
   _____
   _____

2. As the greatest revelation of God's love, what picture of Jesus or Him crucified gave you the assurance of salvation today?

   _____
   _____
   _____
   _____

3. In light of your assurance in Christ, what did the Holy Spirit say to you or ask you to do?

   _____
   _____
   _____
   _____

4. Based on what He said, write at least one verse you will meditate on and memorize today?

   _____
   _____
   _____
   _____

Date: _____ Song: _____ Today's Scripture: _____

1. Tell God what you saw in His character of love.
   _____
   _____
   _____
   _____

2. As the greatest revelation of God's love, what picture of Jesus or Him crucified gave you the assurance of salvation today?
   _____
   _____
   _____
   _____

3. In light of your assurance in Christ, what did the Holy Spirit say to you or ask you to do?
   _____
   _____
   _____
   _____

4. Based on what He said, write at least one verse you will meditate on and memorize today?
   _____
   _____
   _____
   _____

Date: _____ Song: _____ Today's Scripture: _____

1. Tell God what you saw in His character of love.

   _____
   _____
   _____
   _____

2. As the greatest revelation of God's love, what picture of Jesus or Him crucified gave you the assurance of salvation today?

   _____
   _____
   _____
   _____

3. In light of your assurance in Christ, what did the Holy Spirit say to you or ask you to do?

   _____
   _____
   _____
   _____

4. Based on what He said, write at least one verse you will meditate on and memorize today?

   _____
   _____
   _____
   _____

Date: _____ Song: _____ Today's Scripture: _____

1. Tell God what you saw in His character of love.

   _____
   _____
   _____
   _____

2. As the greatest revelation of God's love, what picture of Jesus or Him crucified gave you the assurance of salvation today?

   _____
   _____
   _____
   _____

3. In light of your assurance in Christ, what did the Holy Spirit say to you or ask you to do?

   _____
   _____
   _____
   _____

4. Based on what He said, write at least one verse you will meditate on and memorize today?

   _____
   _____
   _____
   _____

Date: _____ Song: _____ Today's Scripture: _____

1. Tell God what you saw in His character of love.

   _____
   _____
   _____
   _____

2. As the greatest revelation of God's love, what picture of Jesus or Him crucified gave you the assurance of salvation today?

   _____
   _____
   _____
   _____

3. In light of your assurance in Christ, what did the Holy Spirit say to you or ask you to do?

   _____
   _____
   _____
   _____

4. Based on what He said, write at least one verse you will meditate on and memorize today?

   _____
   _____
   _____
   _____

Date: _____ Song: _____ Today's Scripture: _____

1. Tell God what you saw in His character of love.
   _____
   _____
   _____
   _____

2. As the greatest revelation of God's love, what picture of Jesus or Him crucified gave you the assurance of salvation today?
   _____
   _____
   _____
   _____

3. In light of your assurance in Christ, what did the Holy Spirit say to you or ask you to do?
   _____
   _____
   _____
   _____

4. Based on what He said, write at least one verse you will meditate on and memorize today?
   _____
   _____
   _____
   _____

Date: _____ Song: _____ Today's Scripture: _____

1. Tell God what you saw in His character of love.

   _____
   _____
   _____
   _____

2. As the greatest revelation of God's love, what picture of Jesus or Him crucified gave you the assurance of salvation today?

   _____
   _____
   _____
   _____

3. In light of your assurance in Christ, what did the Holy Spirit say to you or ask you to do?

   _____
   _____
   _____
   _____

4. Based on what He said, write at least one verse you will meditate on and memorize today?

   _____
   _____
   _____
   _____

Date: _____ Song: _____ Today's Scripture: _____

1. Tell God what you saw in His character of love.

   _____
   _____
   _____
   _____

2. As the greatest revelation of God's love, what picture of Jesus or Him crucified gave you the assurance of salvation today?

   _____
   _____
   _____
   _____

3. In light of your assurance in Christ, what did the Holy Spirit say to you or ask you to do?

   _____
   _____
   _____
   _____

4. Based on what He said, write at least one verse you will meditate on and memorize today?

   _____
   _____
   _____
   _____

Date: _____ Song: _____ Today's Scripture: _____

1. Tell God what you saw in His character of love.

   _____
   _____
   _____
   _____

2. As the greatest revelation of God's love, what picture of Jesus or Him crucified gave you the assurance of salvation today?

   _____
   _____
   _____
   _____

3. In light of your assurance in Christ, what did the Holy Spirit say to you or ask you to do?

   _____
   _____
   _____
   _____

4. Based on what He said, write at least one verse you will meditate on and memorize today?

   _____
   _____
   _____
   _____

Date: _____ Song: _____ Today's Scripture: _____

1. Tell God what you saw in His character of love.
   _____
   _____
   _____
   _____

2. As the greatest revelation of God's love, what picture of Jesus or Him crucified gave you the assurance of salvation today?
   _____
   _____
   _____
   _____

3. In light of your assurance in Christ, what did the Holy Spirit say to you or ask you to do?
   _____
   _____
   _____
   _____

4. Based on what He said, write at least one verse you will meditate on and memorize today?
   _____
   _____
   _____
   _____

Date: _____ Song: _____ Today's Scripture: _____

1. Tell God what you saw in His character of love.

   _____
   _____
   _____
   _____

2. As the greatest revelation of God's love, what picture of Jesus or Him crucified gave you the assurance of salvation today?

   _____
   _____
   _____
   _____

3. In light of your assurance in Christ, what did the Holy Spirit say to you or ask you to do?

   _____
   _____
   _____
   _____

4. Based on what He said, write at least one verse you will meditate on and memorize today?

   _____
   _____
   _____
   _____

Date: _____ Song: _____ Today's Scripture: _____

1. Tell God what you saw in His character of love.

   _____
   _____
   _____
   _____

2. As the greatest revelation of God's love, what picture of Jesus or Him crucified gave you the assurance of salvation today?

   _____
   _____
   _____
   _____

3. In light of your assurance in Christ, what did the Holy Spirit say to you or ask you to do?

   _____
   _____
   _____
   _____

4. Based on what He said, write at least one verse you will meditate on and memorize today?

   _____
   _____
   _____
   _____

Date: _____ Song: _____ Today's Scripture: _____

1. Tell God what you saw in His character of love.

   _____
   _____
   _____
   _____

2. As the greatest revelation of God's love, what picture of Jesus or Him crucified gave you the assurance of salvation today?

   _____
   _____
   _____
   _____

3. In light of your assurance in Christ, what did the Holy Spirit say to you or ask you to do?

   _____
   _____
   _____
   _____

4. Based on what He said, write at least one verse you will meditate on and memorize today?

   _____
   _____
   _____
   _____

Date: _____ Song: _____ Today's Scripture: _____

1. Tell God what you saw in His character of love.
   _____
   _____
   _____
   _____

2. As the greatest revelation of God's love, what picture of Jesus or Him crucified gave you the assurance of salvation today?
   _____
   _____
   _____
   _____

3. In light of your assurance in Christ, what did the Holy Spirit say to you or ask you to do?
   _____
   _____
   _____
   _____

4. Based on what He said, write at least one verse you will meditate on and memorize today?
   _____
   _____
   _____
   _____

Date: _____ Song: _____ Today's Scripture: _____

1. Tell God what you saw in His character of love.

   _____
   _____
   _____
   _____

2. As the greatest revelation of God's love, what picture of Jesus or Him crucified gave you the assurance of salvation today?

   _____
   _____
   _____
   _____

3. In light of your assurance in Christ, what did the Holy Spirit say to you or ask you to do?

   _____
   _____
   _____
   _____

4. Based on what He said, write at least one verse you will meditate on and memorize today?

   _____
   _____
   _____
   _____

Date: _____ Song: _____ Today's Scripture: _____

1. Tell God what you saw in His character of love.
   _____
   _____
   _____
   _____

2. As the greatest revelation of God's love, what picture of Jesus or Him crucified gave you the assurance of salvation today?
   _____
   _____
   _____
   _____

3. In light of your assurance in Christ, what did the Holy Spirit say to you or ask you to do?
   _____
   _____
   _____
   _____

4. Based on what He said, write at least one verse you will meditate on and memorize today?
   _____
   _____
   _____
   _____

Date: _____ Song: _____ Today's Scripture: _____

1. Tell God what you saw in His character of love.

   _____
   _____
   _____
   _____

2. As the greatest revelation of God's love, what picture of Jesus or Him crucified gave you the assurance of salvation today?

   _____
   _____
   _____
   _____

3. In light of your assurance in Christ, what did the Holy Spirit say to you or ask you to do?

   _____
   _____
   _____
   _____

4. Based on what He said, write at least one verse you will meditate on and memorize today?

   _____
   _____
   _____
   _____

Date: _____ Song: _____ Today's Scripture: _____

1. Tell God what you saw in His character of love.

   _____
   _____
   _____
   _____

2. As the greatest revelation of God's love, what picture of Jesus or Him crucified gave you the assurance of salvation today?

   _____
   _____
   _____
   _____

3. In light of your assurance in Christ, what did the Holy Spirit say to you or ask you to do?

   _____
   _____
   _____
   _____

4. Based on what He said, write at least one verse you will meditate on and memorize today?

   _____
   _____
   _____
   _____

Date: _____ Song: _____ Today's Scripture: _____

1. Tell God what you saw in His character of love.

   _____
   _____
   _____
   _____

2. As the greatest revelation of God's love, what picture of Jesus or Him crucified gave you the assurance of salvation today?

   _____
   _____
   _____
   _____

3. In light of your assurance in Christ, what did the Holy Spirit say to you or ask you to do?

   _____
   _____
   _____
   _____

4. Based on what He said, write at least one verse you will meditate on and memorize today?

   _____
   _____
   _____
   _____

Date: _____ Song: _____ Today's Scripture: _____

1. Tell God what you saw in His character of love.
   _____
   _____
   _____
   _____

2. As the greatest revelation of God's love, what picture of Jesus or Him crucified gave you the assurance of salvation today?
   _____
   _____
   _____
   _____

3. In light of your assurance in Christ, what did the Holy Spirit say to you or ask you to do?
   _____
   _____
   _____
   _____

4. Based on what He said, write at least one verse you will meditate on and memorize today?
   _____
   _____
   _____
   _____

Date: _____ Song: _____ Today's Scripture: _____

1. Tell God what you saw in His character of love.

   _____
   _____
   _____
   _____

2. As the greatest revelation of God's love, what picture of Jesus or Him crucified gave you the assurance of salvation today?

   _____
   _____
   _____
   _____

3. In light of your assurance in Christ, what did the Holy Spirit say to you or ask you to do?

   _____
   _____
   _____
   _____

4. Based on what He said, write at least one verse you will meditate on and memorize today?

   _____
   _____
   _____
   _____

Date: _____ Song: _____ Today's Scripture: _____

1. Tell God what you saw in His character of love.

   _____
   _____
   _____
   _____

2. As the greatest revelation of God's love, what picture of Jesus or Him crucified gave you the assurance of salvation today?

   _____
   _____
   _____
   _____

3. In light of your assurance in Christ, what did the Holy Spirit say to you or ask you to do?

   _____
   _____
   _____
   _____

4. Based on what He said, write at least one verse you will meditate on and memorize today?

   _____
   _____
   _____
   _____

Date: _____ Song: _____ Today's Scripture: _____

1. Tell God what you saw in His character of love.

   _____
   _____
   _____
   _____

2. As the greatest revelation of God's love, what picture of Jesus or Him crucified gave you the assurance of salvation today?

   _____
   _____
   _____
   _____

3. In light of your assurance in Christ, what did the Holy Spirit say to you or ask you to do?

   _____
   _____
   _____
   _____

4. Based on what He said, write at least one verse you will meditate on and memorize today?

   _____
   _____
   _____
   _____

Date: _____ Song: _____ Today's Scripture: _____

1. Tell God what you saw in His character of love.

   _____
   _____
   _____
   _____

2. As the greatest revelation of God's love, what picture of Jesus or Him crucified gave you the assurance of salvation today?

   _____
   _____
   _____
   _____

3. In light of your assurance in Christ, what did the Holy Spirit say to you or ask you to do?

   _____
   _____
   _____
   _____

4. Based on what He said, write at least one verse you will meditate on and memorize today?

   _____
   _____
   _____
   _____

Date: _____ Song: _____ Today's Scripture: _____

1. Tell God what you saw in His character of love.

   _____
   _____
   _____
   _____

2. As the greatest revelation of God's love, what picture of Jesus or Him crucified gave you the assurance of salvation today?

   _____
   _____
   _____
   _____

3. In light of your assurance in Christ, what did the Holy Spirit say to you or ask you to do?

   _____
   _____
   _____
   _____

4. Based on what He said, write at least one verse you will meditate on and memorize today?

   _____
   _____
   _____
   _____

Date: _____ Song: _____ Today's Scripture: _____

1. Tell God what you saw in His character of love.

   _____
   _____
   _____
   _____

2. As the greatest revelation of God's love, what picture of Jesus or Him crucified gave you the assurance of salvation today?

   _____
   _____
   _____
   _____

3. In light of your assurance in Christ, what did the Holy Spirit say to you or ask you to do?

   _____
   _____
   _____
   _____

4. Based on what He said, write at least one verse you will meditate on and memorize today?

   _____
   _____
   _____
   _____

Date: _____ Song: _____ Today's Scripture: _____

1. Tell God what you saw in His character of love.

   _____
   _____
   _____
   _____

2. As the greatest revelation of God's love, what picture of Jesus or Him crucified gave you the assurance of salvation today?

   _____
   _____
   _____
   _____

3. In light of your assurance in Christ, what did the Holy Spirit say to you or ask you to do?

   _____
   _____
   _____
   _____

4. Based on what He said, write at least one verse you will meditate on and memorize today?

   _____
   _____
   _____
   _____

Date: _____ Song: _____ Today's Scripture: _____

1. Tell God what you saw in His character of love.
   _____
   _____
   _____
   _____

2. As the greatest revelation of God's love, what picture of Jesus or Him crucified gave you the assurance of salvation today?
   _____
   _____
   _____
   _____

3. In light of your assurance in Christ, what did the Holy Spirit say to you or ask you to do?
   _____
   _____
   _____
   _____

4. Based on what He said, write at least one verse you will meditate on and memorize today?
   _____
   _____
   _____
   _____

Date: _____ Song: _____ Today's Scripture: _____

1. Tell God what you saw in His character of love.

   _____
   _____
   _____
   _____

2. As the greatest revelation of God's love, what picture of Jesus or Him crucified gave you the assurance of salvation today?

   _____
   _____
   _____
   _____

3. In light of your assurance in Christ, what did the Holy Spirit say to you or ask you to do?

   _____
   _____
   _____
   _____

4. Based on what He said, write at least one verse you will meditate on and memorize today?

   _____
   _____
   _____
   _____

Date: _____ Song: _____ Today's Scripture: _____

1. Tell God what you saw in His character of love.

   _____
   _____
   _____
   _____

2. As the greatest revelation of God's love, what picture of Jesus or Him crucified gave you the assurance of salvation today?

   _____
   _____
   _____
   _____

3. In light of your assurance in Christ, what did the Holy Spirit say to you or ask you to do?

   _____
   _____
   _____
   _____

4. Based on what He said, write at least one verse you will meditate on and memorize today?

   _____
   _____
   _____
   _____

Date: _____ Song: _____ Today's Scripture: _____

1. Tell God what you saw in His character of love.

   _____
   _____
   _____
   _____

2. As the greatest revelation of God's love, what picture of Jesus or Him crucified gave you the assurance of salvation today?

   _____
   _____
   _____
   _____

3. In light of your assurance in Christ, what did the Holy Spirit say to you or ask you to do?

   _____
   _____
   _____
   _____

4. Based on what He said, write at least one verse you will meditate on and memorize today?

   _____
   _____
   _____
   _____

Date: _____ Song: _____ Today's Scripture: _____

1. Tell God what you saw in His character of love.

   _____
   _____
   _____
   _____

2. As the greatest revelation of God's love, what picture of Jesus or Him crucified gave you the assurance of salvation today?

   _____
   _____
   _____
   _____

3. In light of your assurance in Christ, what did the Holy Spirit say to you or ask you to do?

   _____
   _____
   _____
   _____

4. Based on what He said, write at least one verse you will meditate on and memorize today?

   _____
   _____
   _____
   _____

Date: _____ Song: _____ Today's Scripture: _____

1. Tell God what you saw in His character of love.

   _____
   _____
   _____
   _____

2. As the greatest revelation of God's love, what picture of Jesus or Him crucified gave you the assurance of salvation today?

   _____
   _____
   _____
   _____

3. In light of your assurance in Christ, what did the Holy Spirit say to you or ask you to do?

   _____
   _____
   _____
   _____

4. Based on what He said, write at least one verse you will meditate on and memorize today?

   _____
   _____
   _____
   _____

Date: _____ Song: _____ Today's Scripture: _____

1. Tell God what you saw in His character of love.
   _____
   _____
   _____
   _____

2. As the greatest revelation of God's love, what picture of Jesus or Him crucified gave you the assurance of salvation today?
   _____
   _____
   _____
   _____

3. In light of your assurance in Christ, what did the Holy Spirit say to you or ask you to do?
   _____
   _____
   _____
   _____

4. Based on what He said, write at least one verse you will meditate on and memorize today?
   _____
   _____
   _____
   _____

Date: _____ Song: _____ Today's Scripture: _____

1. Tell God what you saw in His character of love.

   _____
   _____
   _____
   _____

2. As the greatest revelation of God's love, what picture of Jesus or Him crucified gave you the assurance of salvation today?

   _____
   _____
   _____
   _____

3. In light of your assurance in Christ, what did the Holy Spirit say to you or ask you to do?

   _____
   _____
   _____
   _____

4. Based on what He said, write at least one verse you will meditate on and memorize today?

   _____
   _____
   _____
   _____

Date: _____ Song: _____ Today's Scripture: _____

1. Tell God what you saw in His character of love.

   _____
   _____
   _____
   _____

2. As the greatest revelation of God's love, what picture of Jesus or Him crucified gave you the assurance of salvation today?

   _____
   _____
   _____
   _____

3. In light of your assurance in Christ, what did the Holy Spirit say to you or ask you to do?

   _____
   _____
   _____
   _____

4. Based on what He said, write at least one verse you will meditate on and memorize today?

   _____
   _____
   _____
   _____

Date: _____ Song: _____ Today's Scripture: _____

1. Tell God what you saw in His character of love.

   _____
   _____
   _____
   _____

2. As the greatest revelation of God's love, what picture of Jesus or Him crucified gave you the assurance of salvation today?

   _____
   _____
   _____
   _____

3. In light of your assurance in Christ, what did the Holy Spirit say to you or ask you to do?

   _____
   _____
   _____
   _____

4. Based on what He said, write at least one verse you will meditate on and memorize today?

   _____
   _____
   _____
   _____

Date: _____ Song: _____ Today's Scripture: _____

1. Tell God what you saw in His character of love.

   _____
   _____
   _____
   _____

2. As the greatest revelation of God's love, what picture of Jesus or Him crucified gave you the assurance of salvation today?

   _____
   _____
   _____
   _____

3. In light of your assurance in Christ, what did the Holy Spirit say to you or ask you to do?

   _____
   _____
   _____
   _____

4. Based on what He said, write at least one verse you will meditate on and memorize today?

   _____
   _____
   _____
   _____

Date: _____ Song: _____ Today's Scripture: _____

1. Tell God what you saw in His character of love.

   _____
   _____
   _____
   _____

2. As the greatest revelation of God's love, what picture of Jesus or Him crucified gave you the assurance of salvation today?

   _____
   _____
   _____
   _____

3. In light of your assurance in Christ, what did the Holy Spirit say to you or ask you to do?

   _____
   _____
   _____
   _____

4. Based on what He said, write at least one verse you will meditate on and memorize today?

   _____
   _____
   _____
   _____

Date: _____ Song: _____ Today's Scripture: _____

1. Tell God what you saw in His character of love.

   _____
   _____
   _____
   _____

2. As the greatest revelation of God's love, what picture of Jesus or Him crucified gave you the assurance of salvation today?

   _____
   _____
   _____
   _____

3. In light of your assurance in Christ, what did the Holy Spirit say to you or ask you to do?

   _____
   _____
   _____
   _____

4. Based on what He said, write at least one verse you will meditate on and memorize today?

   _____
   _____
   _____
   _____

Date: _____ Song: _____ Today's Scripture: _____

1. Tell God what you saw in His character of love.

   _____
   _____
   _____
   _____

2. As the greatest revelation of God's love, what picture of Jesus or Him crucified gave you the assurance of salvation today?

   _____
   _____
   _____
   _____

3. In light of your assurance in Christ, what did the Holy Spirit say to you or ask you to do?

   _____
   _____
   _____
   _____

4. Based on what He said, write at least one verse you will meditate on and memorize today?

   _____
   _____
   _____
   _____

Date: _____ Song: _____ Today's Scripture: _____

1. Tell God what you saw in His character of love.
   _____
   _____
   _____
   _____

2. As the greatest revelation of God's love, what picture of Jesus or Him crucified gave you the assurance of salvation today?
   _____
   _____
   _____
   _____

3. In light of your assurance in Christ, what did the Holy Spirit say to you or ask you to do?
   _____
   _____
   _____
   _____

4. Based on what He said, write at least one verse you will meditate on and memorize today?
   _____
   _____
   _____
   _____

Date: _____ Song: _____ Today's Scripture: _____

1. Tell God what you saw in His character of love.

   _____
   _____
   _____
   _____

2. As the greatest revelation of God's love, what picture of Jesus or Him crucified gave you the assurance of salvation today?

   _____
   _____
   _____
   _____

3. In light of your assurance in Christ, what did the Holy Spirit say to you or ask you to do?

   _____
   _____
   _____
   _____

4. Based on what He said, write at least one verse you will meditate on and memorize today?

   _____
   _____
   _____
   _____

Date: _____ Song: _____ Today's Scripture: _____

1. Tell God what you saw in His character of love.

   _____
   _____
   _____
   _____

2. As the greatest revelation of God's love, what picture of Jesus or Him crucified gave you the assurance of salvation today?

   _____
   _____
   _____
   _____

3. In light of your assurance in Christ, what did the Holy Spirit say to you or ask you to do?

   _____
   _____
   _____
   _____

4. Based on what He said, write at least one verse you will meditate on and memorize today?

   _____
   _____
   _____
   _____

Date: _____ Song: _____ Today's Scripture: _____

1. Tell God what you saw in His character of love.

   _____
   _____
   _____
   _____

2. As the greatest revelation of God's love, what picture of Jesus or Him crucified gave you the assurance of salvation today?

   _____
   _____
   _____
   _____

3. In light of your assurance in Christ, what did the Holy Spirit say to you or ask you to do?

   _____
   _____
   _____
   _____

4. Based on what He said, write at least one verse you will meditate on and memorize today?

   _____
   _____
   _____
   _____

Date: _____ Song: _____ Today's Scripture: _____

1. Tell God what you saw in His character of love.

   _____
   _____
   _____
   _____

2. As the greatest revelation of God's love, what picture of Jesus or Him crucified gave you the assurance of salvation today?

   _____
   _____
   _____
   _____

3. In light of your assurance in Christ, what did the Holy Spirit say to you or ask you to do?

   _____
   _____
   _____
   _____

4. Based on what He said, write at least one verse you will meditate on and memorize today?

   _____
   _____
   _____
   _____

Date: _____ Song: _____ Today's Scripture: _____

1. Tell God what you saw in His character of love.

   _____
   _____
   _____
   _____

2. As the greatest revelation of God's love, what picture of Jesus or Him crucified gave you the assurance of salvation today?

   _____
   _____
   _____
   _____

3. In light of your assurance in Christ, what did the Holy Spirit say to you or ask you to do?

   _____
   _____
   _____
   _____

4. Based on what He said, write at least one verse you will meditate on and memorize today?

   _____
   _____
   _____
   _____

Date: _____ Song: _____ Today's Scripture: _____

1. Tell God what you saw in His character of love.

   _____
   _____
   _____
   _____

2. As the greatest revelation of God's love, what picture of Jesus or Him crucified gave you the assurance of salvation today?

   _____
   _____
   _____
   _____

3. In light of your assurance in Christ, what did the Holy Spirit say to you or ask you to do?

   _____
   _____
   _____
   _____

4. Based on what He said, write at least one verse you will meditate on and memorize today?

   _____
   _____
   _____
   _____

Date: _____ Song: _____ Today's Scripture: _____

1. Tell God what you saw in His character of love.

   _____
   _____
   _____
   _____

2. As the greatest revelation of God's love, what picture of Jesus or Him crucified gave you the assurance of salvation today?

   _____
   _____
   _____
   _____

3. In light of your assurance in Christ, what did the Holy Spirit say to you or ask you to do?

   _____
   _____
   _____
   _____

4. Based on what He said, write at least one verse you will meditate on and memorize today?

   _____
   _____
   _____
   _____

Date: _____ Song: _____ Today's Scripture: _____

1. Tell God what you saw in His character of love.

   _____
   _____
   _____
   _____

2. As the greatest revelation of God's love, what picture of Jesus or Him crucified gave you the assurance of salvation today?

   _____
   _____
   _____
   _____

3. In light of your assurance in Christ, what did the Holy Spirit say to you or ask you to do?

   _____
   _____
   _____
   _____

4. Based on what He said, write at least one verse you will meditate on and memorize today?

   _____
   _____
   _____
   _____

Date: _____ Song: _____ Today's Scripture: _____

1. Tell God what you saw in His character of love.

   _____
   _____
   _____
   _____

2. As the greatest revelation of God's love, what picture of Jesus or Him crucified gave you the assurance of salvation today?

   _____
   _____
   _____
   _____

3. In light of your assurance in Christ, what did the Holy Spirit say to you or ask you to do?

   _____
   _____
   _____
   _____

4. Based on what He said, write at least one verse you will meditate on and memorize today?

   _____
   _____
   _____
   _____

Date: _____ Song: _____ Today's Scripture: _____

1. Tell God what you saw in His character of love.

   _____
   _____
   _____
   _____

2. As the greatest revelation of God's love, what picture of Jesus or Him crucified gave you the assurance of salvation today?

   _____
   _____
   _____
   _____

3. In light of your assurance in Christ, what did the Holy Spirit say to you or ask you to do?

   _____
   _____
   _____
   _____

4. Based on what He said, write at least one verse you will meditate on and memorize today?

   _____
   _____
   _____
   _____

Date: _____ Song: _____ Today's Scripture: _____

1. Tell God what you saw in His character of love.

   _____
   _____
   _____
   _____

2. As the greatest revelation of God's love, what picture of Jesus or Him crucified gave you the assurance of salvation today?

   _____
   _____
   _____
   _____

3. In light of your assurance in Christ, what did the Holy Spirit say to you or ask you to do?

   _____
   _____
   _____
   _____

4. Based on what He said, write at least one verse you will meditate on and memorize today?

   _____
   _____
   _____
   _____

Date: _____ Song: _____ Today's Scripture: _____

1. Tell God what you saw in His character of love.
   _____
   _____
   _____
   _____

2. As the greatest revelation of God's love, what picture of Jesus or Him crucified gave you the assurance of salvation today?
   _____
   _____
   _____
   _____

3. In light of your assurance in Christ, what did the Holy Spirit say to you or ask you to do?
   _____
   _____
   _____
   _____

4. Based on what He said, write at least one verse you will meditate on and memorize today?
   _____
   _____
   _____
   _____

Date: _____ Song: _____ Today's Scripture: _____

1. Tell God what you saw in His character of love.

   _____
   _____
   _____
   _____

2. As the greatest revelation of God's love, what picture of Jesus or Him crucified gave you the assurance of salvation today?

   _____
   _____
   _____
   _____

3. In light of your assurance in Christ, what did the Holy Spirit say to you or ask you to do?

   _____
   _____
   _____
   _____

4. Based on what He said, write at least one verse you will meditate on and memorize today?

   _____
   _____
   _____
   _____

Date: _____ Song: _____ Today's Scripture: _____

1. Tell God what you saw in His character of love.
   _____
   _____
   _____
   _____

2. As the greatest revelation of God's love, what picture of Jesus or Him crucified gave you the assurance of salvation today?
   _____
   _____
   _____
   _____

3. In light of your assurance in Christ, what did the Holy Spirit say to you or ask you to do?
   _____
   _____
   _____
   _____

4. Based on what He said, write at least one verse you will meditate on and memorize today?
   _____
   _____
   _____
   _____

Date: _____ Song: _____ Today's Scripture: _____

1. Tell God what you saw in His character of love.

   _____
   _____
   _____
   _____

2. As the greatest revelation of God's love, what picture of Jesus or Him crucified gave you the assurance of salvation today?

   _____
   _____
   _____
   _____

3. In light of your assurance in Christ, what did the Holy Spirit say to you or ask you to do?

   _____
   _____
   _____
   _____

4. Based on what He said, write at least one verse you will meditate on and memorize today?

   _____
   _____
   _____
   _____

Date: _____ Song: _____ Today's Scripture: _____

1. Tell God what you saw in His character of love.
   _____
   _____
   _____
   _____

2. As the greatest revelation of God's love, what picture of Jesus or Him crucified gave you the assurance of salvation today?
   _____
   _____
   _____
   _____

3. In light of your assurance in Christ, what did the Holy Spirit say to you or ask you to do?
   _____
   _____
   _____
   _____

4. Based on what He said, write at least one verse you will meditate on and memorize today?
   _____
   _____
   _____
   _____

Date: _____ Song: _____ Today's Scripture: _____

1. Tell God what you saw in His character of love.

   _____
   _____
   _____
   _____

2. As the greatest revelation of God's love, what picture of Jesus or Him crucified gave you the assurance of salvation today?

   _____
   _____
   _____
   _____

3. In light of your assurance in Christ, what did the Holy Spirit say to you or ask you to do?

   _____
   _____
   _____
   _____

4. Based on what He said, write at least one verse you will meditate on and memorize today?

   _____
   _____
   _____
   _____

Date: _____ Song: _____ Today's Scripture: _____

1. Tell God what you saw in His character of love.
   _____
   _____
   _____
   _____

2. As the greatest revelation of God's love, what picture of Jesus or Him crucified gave you the assurance of salvation today?
   _____
   _____
   _____
   _____

3. In light of your assurance in Christ, what did the Holy Spirit say to you or ask you to do?
   _____
   _____
   _____
   _____

4. Based on what He said, write at least one verse you will meditate on and memorize today?
   _____
   _____
   _____
   _____

Date: _____ Song: _____ Today's Scripture: _____

1. Tell God what you saw in His character of love.

   _____
   _____
   _____
   _____

2. As the greatest revelation of God's love, what picture of Jesus or Him crucified gave you the assurance of salvation today?

   _____
   _____
   _____
   _____

3. In light of your assurance in Christ, what did the Holy Spirit say to you or ask you to do?

   _____
   _____
   _____
   _____

4. Based on what He said, write at least one verse you will meditate on and memorize today?

   _____
   _____
   _____
   _____

Date: _____ Song: _____ Today's Scripture: _____

1. Tell God what you saw in His character of love.

   _____
   _____
   _____
   _____

2. As the greatest revelation of God's love, what picture of Jesus or Him crucified gave you the assurance of salvation today?

   _____
   _____
   _____
   _____

3. In light of your assurance in Christ, what did the Holy Spirit say to you or ask you to do?

   _____
   _____
   _____
   _____

4. Based on what He said, write at least one verse you will meditate on and memorize today?

   _____
   _____
   _____
   _____

Date: _____ Song: _____ Today's Scripture: _____

1. Tell God what you saw in His character of love.

   _____
   _____
   _____
   _____

2. As the greatest revelation of God's love, what picture of Jesus or Him crucified gave you the assurance of salvation today?

   _____
   _____
   _____
   _____

3. In light of your assurance in Christ, what did the Holy Spirit say to you or ask you to do?

   _____
   _____
   _____
   _____

4. Based on what He said, write at least one verse you will meditate on and memorize today?

   _____
   _____
   _____
   _____

Date: _____ Song: _____ Today's Scripture: _____

1. Tell God what you saw in His character of love.
   _____
   _____
   _____
   _____

2. As the greatest revelation of God's love, what picture of Jesus or Him crucified gave you the assurance of salvation today?
   _____
   _____
   _____
   _____

3. In light of your assurance in Christ, what did the Holy Spirit say to you or ask you to do?
   _____
   _____
   _____
   _____

4. Based on what He said, write at least one verse you will meditate on and memorize today?
   _____
   _____
   _____
   _____

Date: _____ Song: _____ Today's Scripture: _____

1. Tell God what you saw in His character of love.

   _____
   _____
   _____
   _____

2. As the greatest revelation of God's love, what picture of Jesus or Him crucified gave you the assurance of salvation today?

   _____
   _____
   _____
   _____

3. In light of your assurance in Christ, what did the Holy Spirit say to you or ask you to do?

   _____
   _____
   _____
   _____

4. Based on what He said, write at least one verse you will meditate on and memorize today?

   _____
   _____
   _____
   _____

Date: _____ Song: _____ Today's Scripture: _____

1. Tell God what you saw in His character of love.

   _____
   _____
   _____
   _____

2. As the greatest revelation of God's love, what picture of Jesus or Him crucified gave you the assurance of salvation today?

   _____
   _____
   _____
   _____

3. In light of your assurance in Christ, what did the Holy Spirit say to you or ask you to do?

   _____
   _____
   _____
   _____

4. Based on what He said, write at least one verse you will meditate on and memorize today?

   _____
   _____
   _____
   _____

Date: _____ Song: _____ Today's Scripture: _____

1. Tell God what you saw in His character of love.

   _____
   _____
   _____
   _____

2. As the greatest revelation of God's love, what picture of Jesus or Him crucified gave you the assurance of salvation today?

   _____
   _____
   _____
   _____

3. In light of your assurance in Christ, what did the Holy Spirit say to you or ask you to do?

   _____
   _____
   _____
   _____

4. Based on what He said, write at least one verse you will meditate on and memorize today?

   _____
   _____
   _____
   _____

Date: _____ Song: _____ Today's Scripture: _____

1. Tell God what you saw in His character of love.

   _____
   _____
   _____
   _____

2. As the greatest revelation of God's love, what picture of Jesus or Him crucified gave you the assurance of salvation today?

   _____
   _____
   _____
   _____

3. In light of your assurance in Christ, what did the Holy Spirit say to you or ask you to do?

   _____
   _____
   _____
   _____

4. Based on what He said, write at least one verse you will meditate on and memorize today?

   _____
   _____
   _____
   _____

Date: _____ Song: _____ Today's Scripture: _____

1. Tell God what you saw in His character of love.

   _____
   _____
   _____
   _____

2. As the greatest revelation of God's love, what picture of Jesus or Him crucified gave you the assurance of salvation today?

   _____
   _____
   _____
   _____

3. In light of your assurance in Christ, what did the Holy Spirit say to you or ask you to do?

   _____
   _____
   _____
   _____

4. Based on what He said, write at least one verse you will meditate on and memorize today?

   _____
   _____
   _____
   _____

Date: _____ Song: _____ Today's Scripture: _____

1. Tell God what you saw in His character of love.

   _____
   _____
   _____
   _____

2. As the greatest revelation of God's love, what picture of Jesus or Him crucified gave you the assurance of salvation today?

   _____
   _____
   _____
   _____

3. In light of your assurance in Christ, what did the Holy Spirit say to you or ask you to do?

   _____
   _____
   _____
   _____

4. Based on what He said, write at least one verse you will meditate on and memorize today?

   _____
   _____
   _____
   _____

Date: _____ Song: _____ Today's Scripture: _____

1. Tell God what you saw in His character of love.

   _____
   _____
   _____
   _____

2. As the greatest revelation of God's love, what picture of Jesus or Him crucified gave you the assurance of salvation today?

   _____
   _____
   _____
   _____

3. In light of your assurance in Christ, what did the Holy Spirit say to you or ask you to do?

   _____
   _____
   _____
   _____

4. Based on what He said, write at least one verse you will meditate on and memorize today?

   _____
   _____
   _____
   _____

Date: _____ Song: _____ Today's Scripture: _____

1. Tell God what you saw in His character of love.
   _____
   _____
   _____
   _____

2. As the greatest revelation of God's love, what picture of Jesus or Him crucified gave you the assurance of salvation today?
   _____
   _____
   _____
   _____

3. In light of your assurance in Christ, what did the Holy Spirit say to you or ask you to do?
   _____
   _____
   _____
   _____

4. Based on what He said, write at least one verse you will meditate on and memorize today?
   _____
   _____
   _____
   _____

Date: _____ Song: _____ Today's Scripture: _____

1. Tell God what you saw in His character of love.

   _____
   _____
   _____
   _____

2. As the greatest revelation of God's love, what picture of Jesus or Him crucified gave you the assurance of salvation today?

   _____
   _____
   _____
   _____

3. In light of your assurance in Christ, what did the Holy Spirit say to you or ask you to do?

   _____
   _____
   _____
   _____

4. Based on what He said, write at least one verse you will meditate on and memorize today?

   _____
   _____
   _____
   _____

Date: _____ Song: _____ Today's Scripture: _____

1. Tell God what you saw in His character of love.

   _____
   _____
   _____
   _____

2. As the greatest revelation of God's love, what picture of Jesus or Him crucified gave you the assurance of salvation today?

   _____
   _____
   _____
   _____

3. In light of your assurance in Christ, what did the Holy Spirit say to you or ask you to do?

   _____
   _____
   _____
   _____

4. Based on what He said, write at least one verse you will meditate on and memorize today?

   _____
   _____
   _____
   _____

Date: _____ Song: _____ Today's Scripture: _____

1. Tell God what you saw in His character of love.

   _____
   _____
   _____
   _____

2. As the greatest revelation of God's love, what picture of Jesus or Him crucified gave you the assurance of salvation today?

   _____
   _____
   _____
   _____

3. In light of your assurance in Christ, what did the Holy Spirit say to you or ask you to do?

   _____
   _____
   _____
   _____

4. Based on what He said, write at least one verse you will meditate on and memorize today?

   _____
   _____
   _____
   _____

Date: _____ Song: _____ Today's Scripture: _____

1. Tell God what you saw in His character of love.
   _____
   _____
   _____
   _____

2. As the greatest revelation of God's love, what picture of Jesus or Him crucified gave you the assurance of salvation today?
   _____
   _____
   _____
   _____

3. In light of your assurance in Christ, what did the Holy Spirit say to you or ask you to do?
   _____
   _____
   _____
   _____

4. Based on what He said, write at least one verse you will meditate on and memorize today?
   _____
   _____
   _____
   _____

Date: _____ Song: _____ Today's Scripture: _____

1. Tell God what you saw in His character of love.

   _____
   _____
   _____
   _____

2. As the greatest revelation of God's love, what picture of Jesus or Him crucified gave you the assurance of salvation today?

   _____
   _____
   _____
   _____

3. In light of your assurance in Christ, what did the Holy Spirit say to you or ask you to do?

   _____
   _____
   _____
   _____

4. Based on what He said, write at least one verse you will meditate on and memorize today?

   _____
   _____
   _____
   _____

Date: _____ Song: _____ Today's Scripture: _____

1. Tell God what you saw in His character of love.
   _____
   _____
   _____
   _____

2. As the greatest revelation of God's love, what picture of Jesus or Him crucified gave you the assurance of salvation today?
   _____
   _____
   _____
   _____

3. In light of your assurance in Christ, what did the Holy Spirit say to you or ask you to do?
   _____
   _____
   _____
   _____

4. Based on what He said, write at least one verse you will meditate on and memorize today?
   _____
   _____
   _____
   _____

Date: _____ Song: _____ Today's Scripture: _____

1. Tell God what you saw in His character of love.

   _____
   _____
   _____
   _____

2. As the greatest revelation of God's love, what picture of Jesus or Him crucified gave you the assurance of salvation today?

   _____
   _____
   _____
   _____

3. In light of your assurance in Christ, what did the Holy Spirit say to you or ask you to do?

   _____
   _____
   _____
   _____

4. Based on what He said, write at least one verse you will meditate on and memorize today?

   _____
   _____
   _____
   _____

Date: _____ Song: _____ Today's Scripture: _____

1. Tell God what you saw in His character of love.
   _____
   _____
   _____
   _____

2. As the greatest revelation of God's love, what picture of Jesus or Him crucified gave you the assurance of salvation today?
   _____
   _____
   _____
   _____

3. In light of your assurance in Christ, what did the Holy Spirit say to you or ask you to do?
   _____
   _____
   _____
   _____

4. Based on what He said, write at least one verse you will meditate on and memorize today?
   _____
   _____
   _____
   _____

Date: _____ Song: _____ Today's Scripture: _____

1. Tell God what you saw in His character of love.

   _____
   _____
   _____
   _____

2. As the greatest revelation of God's love, what picture of Jesus or Him crucified gave you the assurance of salvation today?

   _____
   _____
   _____
   _____

3. In light of your assurance in Christ, what did the Holy Spirit say to you or ask you to do?

   _____
   _____
   _____
   _____

4. Based on what He said, write at least one verse you will meditate on and memorize today?

   _____
   _____
   _____
   _____

Date: _____ Song: _____ Today's Scripture: _____

1. Tell God what you saw in His character of love.

   _____
   _____
   _____
   _____

2. As the greatest revelation of God's love, what picture of Jesus or Him crucified gave you the assurance of salvation today?

   _____
   _____
   _____
   _____

3. In light of your assurance in Christ, what did the Holy Spirit say to you or ask you to do?

   _____
   _____
   _____
   _____

4. Based on what He said, write at least one verse you will meditate on and memorize today?

   _____
   _____
   _____
   _____

Date: _____ Song: _____ Today's Scripture: _____

1. Tell God what you saw in His character of love.

   _____
   _____
   _____
   _____

2. As the greatest revelation of God's love, what picture of Jesus or Him crucified gave you the assurance of salvation today?

   _____
   _____
   _____
   _____

3. In light of your assurance in Christ, what did the Holy Spirit say to you or ask you to do?

   _____
   _____
   _____
   _____

4. Based on what He said, write at least one verse you will meditate on and memorize today?

   _____
   _____
   _____
   _____

Date: _____ Song: _____ Today's Scripture: _____

1. Tell God what you saw in His character of love.

   _____
   _____
   _____
   _____

2. As the greatest revelation of God's love, what picture of Jesus or Him crucified gave you the assurance of salvation today?

   _____
   _____
   _____
   _____

3. In light of your assurance in Christ, what did the Holy Spirit say to you or ask you to do?

   _____
   _____
   _____
   _____

4. Based on what He said, write at least one verse you will meditate on and memorize today?

   _____
   _____
   _____
   _____

Date: _____ Song: _____ Today's Scripture: _____

1. Tell God what you saw in His character of love.

   _____
   _____
   _____
   _____

2. As the greatest revelation of God's love, what picture of Jesus or Him crucified gave you the assurance of salvation today?

   _____
   _____
   _____
   _____

3. In light of your assurance in Christ, what did the Holy Spirit say to you or ask you to do?

   _____
   _____
   _____
   _____

4. Based on what He said, write at least one verse you will meditate on and memorize today?

   _____
   _____
   _____
   _____

Date: _____ Song: _____ Today's Scripture: _____

1. Tell God what you saw in His character of love.

   _____
   _____
   _____
   _____

2. As the greatest revelation of God's love, what picture of Jesus or Him crucified gave you the assurance of salvation today?

   _____
   _____
   _____
   _____

3. In light of your assurance in Christ, what did the Holy Spirit say to you or ask you to do?

   _____
   _____
   _____
   _____

4. Based on what He said, write at least one verse you will meditate on and memorize today?

   _____
   _____
   _____
   _____

Date: _____ Song: _____ Today's Scripture: _____

1. Tell God what you saw in His character of love.

   _____
   _____
   _____
   _____

2. As the greatest revelation of God's love, what picture of Jesus or Him crucified gave you the assurance of salvation today?

   _____
   _____
   _____
   _____

3. In light of your assurance in Christ, what did the Holy Spirit say to you or ask you to do?

   _____
   _____
   _____
   _____

4. Based on what He said, write at least one verse you will meditate on and memorize today?

   _____
   _____
   _____
   _____

Date: _____ Song: _____ Today's Scripture: _____

1. Tell God what you saw in His character of love.
   _____
   _____
   _____
   _____

2. As the greatest revelation of God's love, what picture of Jesus or Him crucified gave you the assurance of salvation today?
   _____
   _____
   _____
   _____

3. In light of your assurance in Christ, what did the Holy Spirit say to you or ask you to do?
   _____
   _____
   _____
   _____

4. Based on what He said, write at least one verse you will meditate on and memorize today?
   _____
   _____
   _____
   _____

Date: _____ Song: _____ Today's Scripture: _____

1. Tell God what you saw in His character of love.

   _____
   _____
   _____
   _____

2. As the greatest revelation of God's love, what picture of Jesus or Him crucified gave you the assurance of salvation today?

   _____
   _____
   _____
   _____

3. In light of your assurance in Christ, what did the Holy Spirit say to you or ask you to do?

   _____
   _____
   _____
   _____

4. Based on what He said, write at least one verse you will meditate on and memorize today?

   _____
   _____
   _____
   _____

Date: _____ Song: _____ Today's Scripture: _____

1. Tell God what you saw in His character of love.
   _____
   _____
   _____
   _____

2. As the greatest revelation of God's love, what picture of Jesus or Him crucified gave you the assurance of salvation today?
   _____
   _____
   _____
   _____

3. In light of your assurance in Christ, what did the Holy Spirit say to you or ask you to do?
   _____
   _____
   _____
   _____

4. Based on what He said, write at least one verse you will meditate on and memorize today?
   _____
   _____
   _____
   _____

Date: _____ Song: _____ Today's Scripture: _____

1. Tell God what you saw in His character of love.

   _____
   _____
   _____
   _____

2. As the greatest revelation of God's love, what picture of Jesus or Him crucified gave you the assurance of salvation today?

   _____
   _____
   _____
   _____

3. In light of your assurance in Christ, what did the Holy Spirit say to you or ask you to do?

   _____
   _____
   _____
   _____

4. Based on what He said, write at least one verse you will meditate on and memorize today?

   _____
   _____
   _____
   _____

Date: _____ Song: _____ Today's Scripture: _____

1. Tell God what you saw in His character of love.

   _____
   _____
   _____
   _____

2. As the greatest revelation of God's love, what picture of Jesus or Him crucified gave you the assurance of salvation today?

   _____
   _____
   _____
   _____

3. In light of your assurance in Christ, what did the Holy Spirit say to you or ask you to do?

   _____
   _____
   _____
   _____

4. Based on what He said, write at least one verse you will meditate on and memorize today?

   _____
   _____
   _____
   _____

Date: _____ Song: _____ Today's Scripture: _____

1. Tell God what you saw in His character of love.

   _____
   _____
   _____
   _____

2. As the greatest revelation of God's love, what picture of Jesus or Him crucified gave you the assurance of salvation today?

   _____
   _____
   _____
   _____

3. In light of your assurance in Christ, what did the Holy Spirit say to you or ask you to do?

   _____
   _____
   _____
   _____

4. Based on what He said, write at least one verse you will meditate on and memorize today?

   _____
   _____
   _____
   _____

Date: _____ Song: _____ Today's Scripture: _____

1. Tell God what you saw in His character of love.
   _____
   _____
   _____
   _____

2. As the greatest revelation of God's love, what picture of Jesus or Him crucified gave you the assurance of salvation today?
   _____
   _____
   _____
   _____

3. In light of your assurance in Christ, what did the Holy Spirit say to you or ask you to do?
   _____
   _____
   _____
   _____

4. Based on what He said, write at least one verse you will meditate on and memorize today?
   _____
   _____
   _____
   _____

Date: _____ Song: _____ Today's Scripture: _____

1. Tell God what you saw in His character of love.

   _____
   _____
   _____
   _____

2. As the greatest revelation of God's love, what picture of Jesus or Him crucified gave you the assurance of salvation today?

   _____
   _____
   _____
   _____

3. In light of your assurance in Christ, what did the Holy Spirit say to you or ask you to do?

   _____
   _____
   _____
   _____

4. Based on what He said, write at least one verse you will meditate on and memorize today?

   _____
   _____
   _____
   _____

Date: _____ Song: _____ Today's Scripture: _____

1. Tell God what you saw in His character of love.

   _____
   _____
   _____
   _____

2. As the greatest revelation of God's love, what picture of Jesus or Him crucified gave you the assurance of salvation today?

   _____
   _____
   _____
   _____

3. In light of your assurance in Christ, what did the Holy Spirit say to you or ask you to do?

   _____
   _____
   _____
   _____

4. Based on what He said, write at least one verse you will meditate on and memorize today?

   _____
   _____
   _____
   _____

Date: _____ Song: _____ Today's Scripture: _____

1. Tell God what you saw in His character of love.

   _____
   _____
   _____
   _____

2. As the greatest revelation of God's love, what picture of Jesus or Him crucified gave you the assurance of salvation today?

   _____
   _____
   _____
   _____

3. In light of your assurance in Christ, what did the Holy Spirit say to you or ask you to do?

   _____
   _____
   _____
   _____

4. Based on what He said, write at least one verse you will meditate on and memorize today?

   _____
   _____
   _____
   _____

Date: _____ Song: _____ Today's Scripture: _____

1. Tell God what you saw in His character of love.

   _____
   _____
   _____
   _____

2. As the greatest revelation of God's love, what picture of Jesus or Him crucified gave you the assurance of salvation today?

   _____
   _____
   _____
   _____

3. In light of your assurance in Christ, what did the Holy Spirit say to you or ask you to do?

   _____
   _____
   _____
   _____

4. Based on what He said, write at least one verse you will meditate on and memorize today?

   _____
   _____
   _____
   _____

Date: _____ Song: _____ Today's Scripture: _____

1. Tell God what you saw in His character of love.

   _____
   _____
   _____
   _____

2. As the greatest revelation of God's love, what picture of Jesus or Him crucified gave you the assurance of salvation today?

   _____
   _____
   _____
   _____

3. In light of your assurance in Christ, what did the Holy Spirit say to you or ask you to do?

   _____
   _____
   _____
   _____

4. Based on what He said, write at least one verse you will meditate on and memorize today?

   _____
   _____
   _____
   _____

Date: _____ Song: _____ Today's Scripture: _____

1. Tell God what you saw in His character of love.

   _____
   _____
   _____
   _____

2. As the greatest revelation of God's love, what picture of Jesus or Him crucified gave you the assurance of salvation today?

   _____
   _____
   _____
   _____

3. In light of your assurance in Christ, what did the Holy Spirit say to you or ask you to do?

   _____
   _____
   _____
   _____

4. Based on what He said, write at least one verse you will meditate on and memorize today?

   _____
   _____
   _____
   _____

Date: _____ Song: _____ Today's Scripture: _____

1. Tell God what you saw in His character of love.

   _____
   _____
   _____
   _____

2. As the greatest revelation of God's love, what picture of Jesus or Him crucified gave you the assurance of salvation today?

   _____
   _____
   _____
   _____

3. In light of your assurance in Christ, what did the Holy Spirit say to you or ask you to do?

   _____
   _____
   _____
   _____

4. Based on what He said, write at least one verse you will meditate on and memorize today?

   _____
   _____
   _____
   _____

Date: _____ Song: _____ Today's Scripture: _____

1. Tell God what you saw in His character of love.

   _____
   _____
   _____
   _____

2. As the greatest revelation of God's love, what picture of Jesus or Him crucified gave you the assurance of salvation today?

   _____
   _____
   _____
   _____

3. In light of your assurance in Christ, what did the Holy Spirit say to you or ask you to do?

   _____
   _____
   _____
   _____

4. Based on what He said, write at least one verse you will meditate on and memorize today?

   _____
   _____
   _____
   _____

Date: _____ Song: _____ Today's Scripture: _____

1. Tell God what you saw in His character of love.

   _____
   _____
   _____
   _____

2. As the greatest revelation of God's love, what picture of Jesus or Him crucified gave you the assurance of salvation today?

   _____
   _____
   _____
   _____

3. In light of your assurance in Christ, what did the Holy Spirit say to you or ask you to do?

   _____
   _____
   _____
   _____

4. Based on what He said, write at least one verse you will meditate on and memorize today?

   _____
   _____
   _____
   _____

Date: _____ Song: _____ Today's Scripture: _____

1. Tell God what you saw in His character of love.

   _____
   _____
   _____
   _____

2. As the greatest revelation of God's love, what picture of Jesus or Him crucified gave you the assurance of salvation today?

   _____
   _____
   _____
   _____

3. In light of your assurance in Christ, what did the Holy Spirit say to you or ask you to do?

   _____
   _____
   _____
   _____

4. Based on what He said, write at least one verse you will meditate on and memorize today?

   _____
   _____
   _____
   _____

Date: _____ Song: _____ Today's Scripture: _____

1. Tell God what you saw in His character of love.

   _____
   _____
   _____
   _____

2. As the greatest revelation of God's love, what picture of Jesus or Him crucified gave you the assurance of salvation today?

   _____
   _____
   _____
   _____

3. In light of your assurance in Christ, what did the Holy Spirit say to you or ask you to do?

   _____
   _____
   _____
   _____

4. Based on what He said, write at least one verse you will meditate on and memorize today?

   _____
   _____
   _____
   _____

Date: _____ Song: _____ Today's Scripture: _____

1. Tell God what you saw in His character of love.

   _____
   _____
   _____
   _____

2. As the greatest revelation of God's love, what picture of Jesus or Him crucified gave you the assurance of salvation today?

   _____
   _____
   _____
   _____

3. In light of your assurance in Christ, what did the Holy Spirit say to you or ask you to do?

   _____
   _____
   _____
   _____

4. Based on what He said, write at least one verse you will meditate on and memorize today?

   _____
   _____
   _____
   _____

Date: _____ Song: _____ Today's Scripture: _____

1. Tell God what you saw in His character of love.

   _____
   _____
   _____
   _____

2. As the greatest revelation of God's love, what picture of Jesus or Him crucified gave you the assurance of salvation today?

   _____
   _____
   _____
   _____

3. In light of your assurance in Christ, what did the Holy Spirit say to you or ask you to do?

   _____
   _____
   _____
   _____

4. Based on what He said, write at least one verse you will meditate on and memorize today?

   _____
   _____
   _____
   _____

Date: _____ Song: _____ Today's Scripture: _____

1. Tell God what you saw in His character of love.

   _____
   _____
   _____
   _____

2. As the greatest revelation of God's love, what picture of Jesus or Him crucified gave you the assurance of salvation today?

   _____
   _____
   _____
   _____

3. In light of your assurance in Christ, what did the Holy Spirit say to you or ask you to do?

   _____
   _____
   _____
   _____

4. Based on what He said, write at least one verse you will meditate on and memorize today?

   _____
   _____
   _____
   _____